Green **Line**
3/4

von
Jon Marks
Alison Wooder

Ernst Klett Verlag
Stuttgart · Leipzig

Liebe Schülerinnen und Schüler,

Gute Englischkenntnisse bedeuten auch gute Grammatikkenntnisse. Mit den Aufgaben in diesem Heft könnt ihr alle bisher gelernten Grammatikthemen nochmals üben und wiederholen und – wenn mal etwas unverstanden blieb – Lücken auffüllen. Die grammatischen Übungen dieses Heftes helfen euch dabei!

Das Heft ist ideal, um die Grammatikpensen aus den Schulbüchern *Green Line 3* und *4* in selbstständiger Einzelarbeit zu festigen und zu vertiefen. Anhand des Lösungsteils am Ende des Heftes könnt ihr eure Lösungen selbstständig überprüfen. Die grammatischen Übungen lassen sich auch begleitend zur Arbeit mit *Green Line 3* und *4* zur Bearbeitung als Hausaufgabe oder zur gezielten Übung bestimmter Grammatikthemen, z. B. als Vorbereitung auf eine Klassenarbeit, einsetzen.

In diesem Heft findet ihr euch leicht zurecht. Die Kapitel folgen dem Kapitelaufbau von *Green Line 3* und *4*.
Ebenso entspricht die Anordnung der einzelnen Übungen der Reihenfolge der Paragraphen im grammatischen Anhang von *Green Line 3* und *4*. Wollt ihr die Regeln zu einem bestimmten Grammatikthema noch mal nachschauen, dann findet ihr rechts oben über jeder Aufgabe einen Verweis z. B. → G1 zu dem entsprechenden Paragraphen im grammatischen Anhang der Schulbücher.

Grammatik ist wichtig und kann auch Spaß machen. *99 grammatische Übungen* bieten abwechslungsreiche und motivierende Aufgabenformen wie Auswahlantworten, Einsetzübungen, Zuordnungsaufgaben und Rätsel. Als besonders motivierenden Teil enthält jedes Kapitel außerdem einen *Cartoon*, der ein bestimmtes Grammatikthema hervorhebt. Viele Aufgaben sind als Dialoge, Briefe oder E-Mails in ansprechende Kontexte eingebettet und bieten authentische und abwechslungsreiche Kommunikationsanlässe. Jedes Kapitel wird durch eine *mixed bag*-Übung abgeschlossen, mit der ihr eure erworbenen Kenntnisse überprüfen könnt.

Viel Erfolg und hoffentlich auch Spaß!

Euer *Green Line* Team

Inhaltsverzeichnis

Unit 1 The world of sport

1 Talking about sport

→ G1

*Complete the sentences. Use **will** or **going to** and the verb in brackets.*

1. We _'re going to play_ (play) football on Saturday. I've phoned the team and everyone can come.
2. Look at Helen! She's a long way behind the others. She ______________ (come) last.
3. There's a big match tomorrow. I hope it ______________. (not rain)
4. Promise me you ______________ (be) careful when you go skateboarding this afternoon.
5. I've bought the tickets! We ______________ (watch) the match on Saturday!
6. John's in the changing rooms at the moment, but I'm sure he ______________ (not be) long.
7. Just look at those black clouds up there. It ______________ (rain) before the match finishes.
8. I don't feel well. I don't think I ______________ (go) to the swimming pool this morning.
9. It's my seventeenth birthday next month. I ______________ (be) old enough to learn to drive.
10. We ______________ (watch) the football match tomorrow. Would you like to come?

2 When does it open?

→ G2

Look at the use of present simple with future meaning. Are these sentences grammatically correct or not? Tick the right box and correct the mistakes.

	correct	not correct
1. The new sports centre opens next week.	☐	☐
2. I can't go shopping this afternoon because I watch the cricket match.	☐	☐
3. Jason meets me at the swimming pool this evening.	☐	☐
4. The swimming pool closes for the winter at the end of September.	☐	☐
5. The bus to the stadium leaves at 10.15 and arrives there at 10.50.	☐	☐
6. I play tennis with Joe this evening.	☐	☐
7. Please hurry up! The train leaves in ten minutes.	☐	☐
8. The last date for students to enter the competition is next Friday.	☐	☐

____

____

____

____

3 Surfing course

→ G3

Helen is going on a surfing course tomorrow. Look at the timetable and Helen's e-mail and complete the gaps with the right present progressive forms. Use short forms ('s, 're …).

Saturday	
9.00 am	leave home[1]/drive to surf school[2]
10.30 am	meet trainer and students[3]
11.00 am	watch video[4]
11.30 am	walk to beach[5]
11.45 am – 1.00 pm	lesson 1 – safety and using your board
1.00 – 1.45 pm	lunch at Windrush Beach Cafe[6]
1.45 pm – 4.30 pm	meet on beach[7] and surf in sea

From: helen@funmail.co.uk
To: jay@funmail.co.uk
Subject: Surfing course

Address book

Hi Jay!

Sorry I can't come shopping with you on Saturday, but I've got a really busy weekend! Liz and I are going on a surfing course. We ______________ [1] home at 9 am on Saturday morning. Dad ______________ [2] us to the surf school. It's very near the sea. Then we ______________ [3] the other people on the course and the trainer at 10.30 for the first part. Then at 11 we ______________ [4] a short video about how to surf. After that we ______________ [5] down to the beach for our first ever surf lesson! This part is just on the beach, showing us how to use the board and be safe. Then I ______________ [6] lunch at a beach cafe called 'Windrush'. After lunch, we ______________ [7] back on the beach before we surf in the sea for the first time! It's going to be great fun.

I'll send you an e-mail telling you all about it when I get back home again.

Lots of love
Helen

4 What was the reply?

→ G4

Match the speakers with the correct responses.

1. My train arrives really late the evening. There won't be any buses and a taxi will be really expensive.
2. I don't think I understand what you said about relative clauses.
3. Is that the phone?
4. I left my dictionary at home.
5. I'm moving house tomorrow. It's going to be really hard work.

a) I'll get it. It's probably for me.
b) We'll come along and help you if you like.
c) I'll explain it again more slowly, then.
d) We'll pick you up in the car if you like.
e) I'll lend you mine, but I need it back again tomorrow.

5 Sports crossword

→ G5

Underline the right relative pronoun to complete these crossword clues. Then do the crossword.

1. This is the person (which/who) decides about points in tennis matches.
2. This is a group of people (–/who) play to win together.
3. This is a piece of equipment (that/what) some sports players wear on their heads.
4. This is a team game (who/which) is popular in India, Australia and Britain.
5. This is someone (who/which) goes down mountains very fast in the snow.
6. This is something (–/what) tennis players use.
7. This is the person (who/–) controls a football game.

6 Sentences with *whose*

→ G6

Use ***whose*** *to make one sentence out of two sentences. Look at the example first.*

1. There's the boy. His brother is an Olympic athlete.
   There's the boy whose brother is an Olympic athlete.
2. Jack Evans is a sports writer. His books have sold over a million copies.
   ____
3. I know a girl. Her grandmother was a very famous tennis player.
   ____
4. There's a boy in my class. His parents teach skiing.
   ____
5. Who's the famous cyclist? I saw his bike outside.
   ____
6. Those are the athletes. Their photos were in the newspaper.
   ____

7 Whose or who's?

→ G6

*Put in **who's** or **whose** to complete the sentences.*

1. That's the man ________________ teaching Paul to ski.
2. This is the girl ________________ brother is in my judo class.
3. Is that the rugby player ________________ in the English team?
4. This is Anna, ________________ an excellent volleyball player.
5. A referee is a person ________________ job is to decide about rules in football matches.
6. Is that the boy ________________ sports bag you borrowed?

8 Which sentence is correct?

→ G7

In each number look at sentence a and b. Which one of them is correct? Tick the right box.

1. a) That's the person I lent my skateboard to. ☐
   b) That's the person to who I lent my skateboard. ☐
2. a) Are those the girls with who you were playing? ☐
   b) Are those the girls you were playing with? ☐
3. a) Did you find the pair of trainers for which you were looking for? ☐
   b) Did you find the pair of trainers you were looking for? ☐
4. a) I didn't see the match you're talking about. ☐
   b) I didn't see the match of which you're talking about. ☐
5. a) Is that the trainer you were talking to earlier? ☐
   b) Is that the trainer were you talking to earlier? ☐
6. a) Can you describe the referee to whom you were speaking? ☐
   b) Can you describe the referee to who you were speaking? ☐

9 Find the mistakes

→ G1, G2, G5

There are two mistakes in every sentence. Underline them and write down the correct version.

1. I think tomorrow's match is being the most exciting match what I've ever seen.

____

2. The advertisement who I saw said that the match is beginning at 2 pm.

____

3. I'm sure that Ellie Evans is the player which wins the most tennis matches next year.

____

10 A cartoon: The spaceship

11 Mixed bag: The charity

Underline the right form of the going-to-future, will-future or the right relative pronoun to complete the dialogue.

John: What (will you do / are you doing) on Sunday next week?

Elena: I'm not sure. Why?

John: Well, there ('s / is being) a big charity fun run. I ('m going to / will) take part in it and I wondered if you'd like to come, too.

Elena: That sounds like a good idea. Which charity is it for?

John: The one (who / which) helps the local hospital. It's called Heartbeat, I think.

Elena: I ('ll / 'm going to) just check in my diary to see if I'm (being / going to be) free then. Hold on a moment.

John: OK.

Elena: So, let's see. Well, on Saturday my cousin (will come / 's coming) to stay for the weekend.

John: Well, that's good. You can ask your cousin to come, too. Which cousin is it?

Elena: It's Jim, the one (who / which) is crazy about football. You met him last year. And yes, you're right – he ('ll be / 's being) happy to run for charity as well. I ('m giving / 'll give) him a ring in a moment and tell him about it. Where does the run begin?

John: Do you know the car park behind the sports centre? (We're all meeting / We'll all meet) there at 10.00.

Elena: Great! I ('m going to see / 'll see) you there!

Unit 2 Once upon a time ...

1 You can and you may ...

→ G8

*Look at the use of **can** and **may** in these sentences and tick the right box.*

	Talking about ability	Talking about what's allowed
1. You may bring your camera into the museum but you can't take photos.		
2. I can't believe anyone actually wore clothes like this.		
3. We can't understand the signs in the museum because they're in French.		
4. May I ask you about this painting of the Globe Theatre, please?		
5. If you like, you can touch the objects in the box.		
6. Move out of the way of that sign, please. I can't read it with you standing there.		
7. I'm afraid you can't bring large bags into the museum.		

2 Correct or not correct?

→ G8

a) *Are these sentences grammatically correct or not? Tick the right box.*

	correct	not correct
1. We really must to hurry up if we want to see everything.	☐	☐
2. The museum guides cans speak many languages.	☐	☐
3. We mustn't be late for the tour of the museum.	☐	☐
4. You can look at the paintings but you don't must touch.	☐	☐
5. We needn't buy tickets because the museum is free on Sundays.	☐	☐
6. When I read that children worked in the factories I didn't can believe it.	☐	☐
7. You may borrow an audio guide if you want to.	☐	☐
8. We wanted to go to the museum but we couldn't find it.	☐	☐
9. Do you can see dinosaurs in the museum?	☐	☐

b) *Now match the mistakes to the grammar rules below. There is one incorrect sentence for each mistake.*

A. Modal auxiliary verbs do not use an *s* in the 3rd person singular. Sentence ______

B. Modal auxiliary verbs do not use *do* or *does* in the question forms. Sentence ______

C. There's no *to* between the auxiliary verb and the main verb. Sentence ______

D. Modal auxiliary verbs do not use *do* or *does* in the negative form. Sentence ______

E. Modal auxiliary verbs do not use *didn't* to make the past form. Sentence ______

3 What are they able to do?

→ G9

Use a form of ***be able to*** *+ verb to complete the sentences. Use the tenses in brackets.*

1. (Simple past:) My parents weren't able to book (not/book) the hotel they wanted because they'd left it too late.
2. (Present perfect:) I'm afraid I ______ (finish) the work this week because I've been too busy getting ready for my holiday.
3. (Will-future:) If you ask Karen I'm sure she ______ (help) you while I'm away.
4. (Simple past:) After his holiday in Paris last year, William ______ (understand) French quite easily.
5. (Present perfect:) I hope Jon ______ (find) his passport.
6. (Will-future:) After our holiday in Mexico we ______ (speak) Spanish very well.
7. (Simple past:) Karl ______ (not/get) tickets for the flight on Saturday.

4 Kim's new school

→ G9

Use a form of ***be allowed to*** *to rewrite the marked sentences.*

"Hi! I changed schools last month. There are lots of differences between my old school and my new school. In my last school, students **couldn't walk**[1] on the grass or play ball games near the school buildings. Now we **can play**[2] where we like! I **couldn't wear**[3] my favourite red shoes in my old school but my new school doesn't have any rules about shoes or other clothes. We **may wear**[4] anything we want. **Can you wear**[5] any clothes you like in your school, too? There's a swimming pool in my new school, so in the summer we **can go**[6] swimming! It's going to be great!"

1. ______
2. ______
3. ______
4. ______
5. ______
6. ______

5 Similar meanings

→ G9

Match the sentences which have a similar meaning.

1. He needn't go inside.
2. He mustn't go inside.
3. He couldn't go inside.
4. He'll be able to go inside.
5. He won't need to go inside.
6. He was able to go inside.

a) It will be possible[1] for him to go inside.
b) He wasn't able to go inside.
c) It was possible for him to go inside.
d) He doesn't have to go inside.
e) He won't have to go inside.
f) He can't go inside.

[1] possible ['pɒsəbl] – möglich

6 Sam's new job

→ G9

Read the e-mail and fill the gaps with a form of ***have to*** *and one of the verbs. Use the tense in brackets.*

go | not pay | not act | learn | practise | answer

From: sam@funmail.co.uk
To: bill@funmail.co.uk
Subject: Job at Globe

Address book

Hi Bill!

You know I had an interview with the Globe Theatre to work there this summer? Well, I got the job!

In my interview I ______________________ (simple past) lots of questions about Shakespeare and the theatre. Tomorrow I ______________________ (will-future) to the museum and choose some clothes to wear for the job. I ______________________ (will-future) for them, which is lucky, because they're very expensive. I'm excited about the job, of course, but a little worried too, because I ______________________ (present perfect) in front of a large group before. I ______________________ (simple present) lots of facts about the Globe so that I can answer people's questions when I start work. I hope I can remember everything. I ______________________ (will-future) a lot.

Speak to you later!
Sam

7 A cartoon: A bad cold

8 A trip to London

→ G9

Finish the sentences with the right form of the modal verb and the verb in brackets.

1. I hope we ______________ the Tower of London next week. (can/visit)
2. When we visited London Zoo last week, we ______________ the animals. (may/feed)
3. I've never ______________ to the Tower of London before, so I'm quite excited. (can/go)
4. You ______________ a map with you on your trip tomorrow. (must/take)
5. I ______________ this trip carefully because I wanted it to be perfect. (must/plan)

9 The city trip

→ G10

Match the halves of the broken sentences.

1. We couldn't find the hotel because ...
2. I didn't take any photos because ...
3. By the time I got to the restaurant ...
4. When I went to take a photo ...
5. I didn't understand the brochure because ...
6. I asked Dave for his old guidebook but ...

a) I remembered I'd forgotten to bring my camera.
b) he'd already thrown it away.
c) we'd left the map behind.
d) I hadn't read it carefully.
e) I'd been there before and had already taken a lot.
f) it had already closed.

10 Past perfect or simple past?

→ G10

Use the simple past or past perfect form of the verbs in brackets to complete these sentences.

1. Peter felt very tired because he hadn't slept well the night before. (feel/not sleep)
2. I already ______________ Tom because I ______________ him a few times before. (know/meet)
3. We ______________ to London Zoo because we ______________ it before. (not go/visit)
4. When I ______________ to the bus stop, my bus ______________ already ______________. (get/leave)
5. I ______________ Lisa was in town because she ______________ me an e-mail a few days before. (know/send)
6. When Jake ______________ at the cafe, Sonia ______________ already ______________ home. (arrive/go)
7. The fridge ______________ full of delicious food because Anna ______________ to the supermarket that morning. (be/be)

11 Mixed bag: Trouble with Grandma

Underline the right form of the past perfect and modal auxiliaries to complete the dialogue.

Grandma: You aren't going out looking like that, are you, Jackie?

Jackie: Why, what's wrong with what I'm wearing, Gran?

Grandma: Well, for one thing, you (won't be able to/haven't been able to) walk in those boots. They're far too high. Did I tell you about the time when I fell over on the ice?

Jackie: Yes, Gran, you did.

Grandma: And when I got to the hospital they told me that I (broke /'d broken) my leg in three different places. I (wasn't able to/hadn't been able to) walk for two months. If you wear high boots like that, you could fall over, too.

Jackie: Oh you (haven't had to/needn't) worry about that! I can walk in much higher boots than this.

Grandma: Well, what about your skirt? You (don't have to/mustn't) go out wearing such a short skirt or you'll catch a cold. You (have to/are allowed to) wear something warmer if you're going out on a cold evening like this.

Jackie: You really (don't have to/haven't to) worry about me, Gran. I won't get cold – I'm only going as far as Eva's house to watch a film on television.

Grandma: When I was your age, I (wasn't allowed to/mustn't) go out with short skirts. I had to wear flat shoes as well.

Jackie: Look, Gran, I'd love to stay and chat, but I really (had to/must) go now. I said I'd be at Eva's in half an hour. Last time I got to her house late and the film (has already/had already) started.

Grandma: Well, have a nice time, dear, and be careful how you walk in those boots!

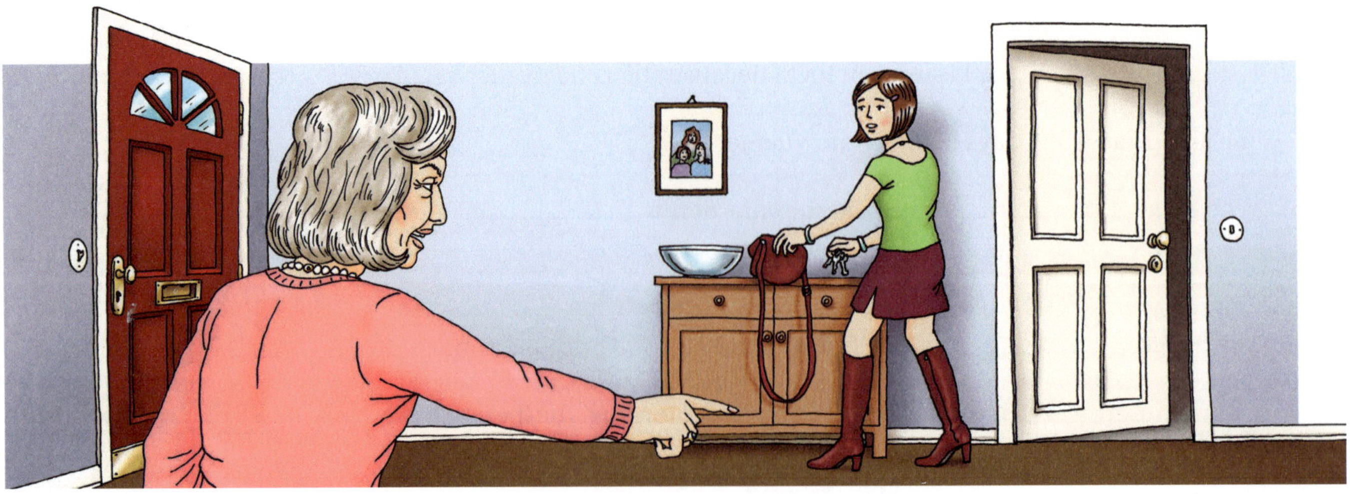

Unit 3 Living together

1 Parties, paint and puppies

→ G11

Complete the dialogue with the right reflexive pronoun.

Sara: My oldest brother Max had a great party last night. He's moved into a new house.

Rebecca: Yes, I heard. Does he live by ________________ now?

Sara: No, he's sharing a house with some student friends. When they first moved in, a few weeks ago, all the walls were painted a horrible orange colour, but now they've made it all look much nicer.

Rebecca: Did they ask a painter to do it?

Sara: No, they painted the place ________________. I thought Max invited you too, so I was surprised you weren't there. It's too bad you didn't come! We really enjoyed ________________!

Rebecca: Yes, I'd have liked to go, but you know we got a new puppy two weeks ago. It's still too small to be left by ________________. It's very young and it misses its mother.

Sara: Oh, poor little thing. Are you planning to take it to dog training classes?

Rebecca: No, there's no need. I'll train it ________________. It's very good. My little cousin Kate came round to visit last week, and she's only three years old, but the dog behaved ________________ all day. It didn't bite or bark at all. Kate didn't behave ________________ though! She wrote on my bedroom wall with my best pens. I couldn't believe it!

2 Correct or not correct?

→ G11

Are these sentences grammatically correct or not? Tick the right box and underline the mistakes.

	correct	not correct
1. You need to sit down and relax yourself.	☐	☐
2. I don't usually look at myself in the mirror when I get dressed myself.	☐	☐
3. Sarah reminded herself not to forget her keys.	☐	☐
4. We have to hurry ourselves up if we don't want to be late.	☐	☐
5. My little brother is too young to dress himself, so I sometimes help him.	☐	☐
6. I've decided myself to teach myself how to play the guitar.	☐	☐
7. When we moved ourselves from the town to the country, everything was quieter.	☐	☐
8. I hope you two boys behaved yourselves this evening.	☐	☐
9. Your sister has changed herself a lot since I last saw her.	☐	☐

3 A crossword

→ G11

Fill in the crossword with the reflexive pronouns that are missing from the sentences.

1. Do you and your husband have a gardener to cut your grass for you? No, we always cut it …
2. Did you help your daughter to tidy her room? No, she tidied it …
3. Can you clean our windows, please? No! Clean them …
4. Where did you buy these curtains? I didn't buy them. I made them …
5. Can you help me find my front door key? Not again! Find it …
6. Do the Robinsons pay someone to clean their windows for them? No, they clean their windows …
7. I love your brother's tree house! Did your dad build it? No, my brother made it …

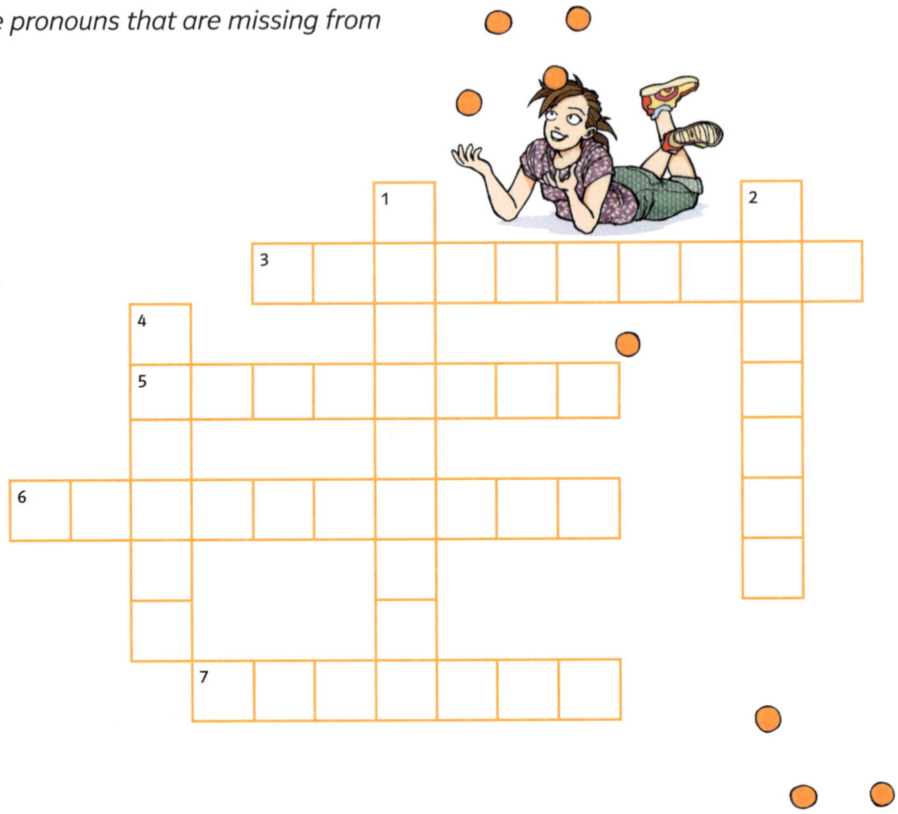

4 Eva's e-mail

→ G11, G12

Complete Eva's e-mail to Jenny with ***yourselves, ourselves, themselves*** *or* ***each other****.*

From: eva@funmail.co.uk
To: jenny@funmail.co.uk
Subject: Holiday

Address book

Hi Jenny!

Thanks for your e-mail last week. Good to hear about your family holiday. I'm glad that you enjoyed ________________ on the beach. Sorry I didn't answer your e-mail until now, but I was away from home. My brother Bill and I stayed with my aunt and uncle in their house in the country. Bill and I took the train to their house by ________________, because my parents were at work. I don't see my cousins very often. We usually only phone ________________ a few times a year, so it was nice for us all to get to know ________________ better.

We enjoyed ________________, but it was sometimes quite difficult because it rained quite a lot and my cousins don't get on very well with ________________. They're always fighting. Once they were arguing when they were riding their bikes, and they both fell off. They didn't hurt ________________ badly, though, so that was OK. We took our dog (who's called Cooper) with us. Our cousins have a dog, too, and the two dogs played with ________________ most of the week. Anyway, it'll be great to see you when we're back at school next week!

Love from Eva

5 Broken sentences

→ G13

Match the halves of the broken sentences.

1. I'll lend you my bike
2. We'll come and help you
3. I'll go crazy
4. I won't mind
5. If Simon phones when I'm out,
6. If we don't hurry up,
7. If it's good weather at the weekend,
8. If you see Amy,

a) … I'll phone him back later.
b) … if you don't want to come along.
c) … if you give it back tomorrow.
d) … will you tell her about the party?
e) … we'll go to the beach.
f) … if the twins don't stop arguing soon.
g) … if you like.
h) … we'll miss the train.

6 What would they do?

→ G13

Form if-clauses type II with the verbs in brackets to complete the sentences.

1. If I ______ the money, I ______ a new phone. (have/buy)
2. If I ______ you, I ______ to bed early. (be/go)
3. If we ______ a party, we ______ everyone in the class. (have/invite)
4. What ______ the teacher ______ if she ______ you using your mobile? (do/see)
5. We ______ outside if it ______ warmer. (sit/be)
6. If your parents ______ for the weekend, ______ you ______ a party? (go away/have)
7. If I ______ how to do it, I ______ my bike myself. (know/mend)
8. Your dad ______ happy if he ______ you were here. (not be/know)

7 What do you wish?

→ G13

Make if-clauses type II for these situations.

1. I can't get the book from the shelf. I'm not tall enough. I wish I was taller.
2. I can't understand this sign. I can't read Russian. ______
3. I want to look up this word. I haven't got a dictionary. ______
4. I don't understand the grammar. The teacher speaks too fast. ______
5. I can't buy a new computer. I haven't got enough money. ______
6. I can't phone Pilar in Spain. I've forgotten my Spanish. ______

8 The school play

→ G13

Phil is phoning his friend Owen. Read the dialogue, then use the verbs in brackets to make if-clauses type III about the situation.

Phil: Hi Owen! It's Phil here. I just phoned to ask how the play went on Saturday evening.
Owen: Hi! It went well, I think. There were lots of times when I thought something was going to go wrong, but in fact, on the night everything was OK.
Phil: What kind of things were you worried about?
Owen: Well, Sue was making the costumes for the play, but she was really slow. I didn't think that she would finish on time, and I was hoping we wouldn't have to do the play in our normal everyday boring clothes. But she finished the night before, in fact, so everything was fine.
Phil: That's good. Did you sell lots of tickets?
Owen: Well, I was worried about that, too. I thought nobody had told people about the show, but Helen made a really good job of that, so on the night we sold all our tickets.
Phil: Great! It's good to have a big audience. How was your acting? Did you remember all your lines?
Owen: Yes, but only because I stayed up all night on Friday learning them. But I didn't forget anything.
Phil: And the other actors? Were they OK?
Owen: Leo said he nearly fell off the stage, because the lights were in his eyes, but luckily he didn't.
Phil: That's lucky! I wish I'd been able to come, but I had to go to my aunt's birthday party instead.

1. If Sue ______________________ (not finish) the costumes, the cast

   ______________________ (have to) wear normal clothes.

2. If nobody ______________________ (tell) people about the show, they

   ______________________ (not sell) all the tickets.

3. If Owen ______________________ (not stay up) all night learning his lines, he

   ______________________ (forget) them.

4. If the lights ______________________ (not be) in his eyes, Leo

   ______________________ nearly ______________________ (not fall) off the stage.

9 A cartoon: Bad luck

10 Mixed bag: A quiz

Underline the correct words to complete the quiz, then answer the questions.

Quiz! How independent are you?

1. If you (would see/saw) a spider in the bath, what would you do?
   - ☐ a) (I'll/I'd) scream and run away.
   - ☐ b) I'd ask my dad to get it out for (me/myself).
   - ☐ c) I'd get it out (myself/itself) without any problem.

2. If you (were/had been) one of a pair of twins, how would you both behave?
   - ☐ a) We'd dress the same as (ourselves/each other) and always do the same things.
   - ☐ b) We'd be close friends but we'd try to do things by (ourselves/ourself) sometimes.
   - ☐ c) We'd try to be as different from (ourselves/each other) as possible.

3. Your friend's computer broke last week. He tried to mend it (alone/himself), but now it doesn't work at all. If your own computer (will break/had broken) down, what would you have done?
   - ☐ a) I'd have asked my parents for a new computer.
   - ☐ b) I'd (take/have taken) it to the computer shop and paid someone to fix it.
   - ☐ c) I'd have fixed it (myself/myselves). It can't be that difficult!

4. If someone (has invited/invited) you and your best friend to a monster party, what (do/would) you do?
   - ☐ a) We'd buy a monster costume from a shop.
   - ☐ b) We'd make masks (ourselves/each other), but we wouldn't spend much time on it.
   - ☐ c) We'd spend a lot of time making the best monster costumes ever.

5. Your friend decided to cut her own hair last week. It looked terrible! If she (would have asked/had asked) your advice, what would you have said?
   - ☐ a) I'd (tell/have told) her to go to a hairdresser.
   - ☐ b) I'd have told her to ask her mum to cut it for her.
   - ☐ c) I'd have cut her hair (myself/for herself).

Unit 4 The UK on the move

1 *The* or no article?

→ G14

Look at the sentences and decide if you need an article or not. Put in ***the*** *or –.*

1. Did the builders finish __________ work on the new bus station?
2. I can't go away for the weekend because I've got __________ too much work.
3. When you're enjoying the journey __________ time seems to get faster.
4. Do you remember __________ time when we were in that museum in Liverpool?
5. We're taking __________ coach to Windsor tomorrow.
6. Travelling by __________ coach is cheaper than travelling by __________ train.
7. I don't usually have anything for __________ breakfast when I stay in hotels.
8. __________ breakfast we had at the hotel this morning was very large.

2 A conversation on a bus

→ G14

Complete the gaps with ***a***, ***an***, ***the*** *or no article (–).*

Helen: Hello, Lucy! I didn't know you took __________ bus to __________ school!

Lucy: Well, usually I walk to school, but today I had to take the bus because I was in __________ hurry. My brother Andy is ill. He had __________ awful headache last night and this morning he's got __________ high temperature.

Helen: Oh no! Did he have to go to __________ hospital?

Lucy: No, my mother called __________ doctor and he told him to go back to __________ bed and call again later.

Helen: Your brother was working as __________ waiter last month, wasn't he?

Lucy: Yes, that's right. He enjoyed working as a waiter but he said it was __________ very hard work. At the moment he's teaching himself how to play __________ piano because he wants to work as __________ musician in __________ same restaurant __________ next summer.

Helen: Really? My mum's __________ piano teacher. If he likes, Andy can come round and speak to her.

Lucy: That would be great. This is our bus stop now. Let's talk about this at __________ lunch today.

3 Famous sayings

→ G15

Here are some sayings in English which use adjectives as nouns. Match the sayings with the explanations.

1. "Never speak ill of the dead."
2. "A word to the wise is enough."
3. "The good die young."
4. "The poor are always with us."
5. "It's one rule for the rich and another for the poor."
6. "In the country of the blind, the one-eyed man is king."

a) Sometimes the best people do not live a long time.
b) You shouldn't say bad things about people after they die.
c) At all times in history there have been poor people.
d) Money changes what you can and can't do.
e) You don't have to explain every detail to intelligent people.
f) When nobody else knows anything about a subject, the person who knows only a little has the most power.

4 Adjectives after verbs

→ G16

Read the dialogue and choose the best verb to fill the gaps. Change the form of the verb if you need to. You can use a verb more than once.

feel | get | seem | smell | sound | stay

Paula: This Friday my brother's band are playing in a big club in town, in a place called Zack's.

Alan: Really? That ________________ interesting. I remember the last time I was at Zack's there'd been a fire. The whole place ________________ terrible. Smoke and burnt carpets.

Paula: Yes, you're right. That was a few years ago. It's much nicer now.

Alan: Your brother must be ________________ pleased that they got a chance to perform at a big place like Zack's. There are always lots of people there on Fridays and Saturdays.

Paula: Yes, he's very pleased about it! His band is ________________ quite famous now. They've been on the radio a few times.

Alan: Does it ________________ strange to hear your own brother on the radio?

Paula: Yes, it ________________ a bit odd at first, but now it just ________________ normal.

Alan: Is your brother worried about standing up in front of lots of people?

Paula: Who, Bill? No way! He never ________________ nervous. But the singer, Jim, doesn't like big audiences. They've been telling Jim to relax and try to ________________ calm.

5 Adverb or adjective?

→ G16

Finish the sentences with an adjective or adverb.

1. Mr Allen looked at his hair ________________ and noticed that it was getting very ________________ as well as grey. (sad/thin)
2. Jake didn't want to be ________________ for school so he got dressed ________________. (late/quick)
3. The dog smelled the air ________________. Something in the kitchen smelled ________________. (happy/delicious)
4. The classroom seems quite ________________ to me, but I'm not feeling ________________ at the moment. Perhaps I'm getting a cold. (cold/fantastic)
5. I looked ________________ at the newspaper story about Liverpool because it looked very ________________. (careful/interesting)
6. This hotel sounds ________________. We could stay there for a few days quite ________________. (good/cheap)
7. Touch the cat's ears ________________. They feel really ________________. (careful/soft)
8. The film Anne and Jules went to see at the cinema seemed ________________ at first, but later it turned out to be really ________________. (boring/exciting)
9. Sarah read the difficult exam ________________, but she managed to stay ________________ and so she passed it. (nervous/calm)

6 A cartoon: Two jokes

7 Henry's plans for the future

→ G17

Henry has a lot of plans for his future. Write down what he thinks he will have done when he's 30. Use the future perfect.

1. I will have got a cool job ______. + get a cool job
2. ______. – earn a million pounds
3. ______. + meet a nice woman
4. ______. – marry
5. ______. + buy a car
6. ______. – buy a house

8 A busy weekend

→ G17

Lee and Jade's parents are away on holiday and they want to surprise them and do some jobs in the house and garden before they get back. They are planning to do lots of things. Look at their plan for the weekend and complete the sentences about what they will have done by this time next week.

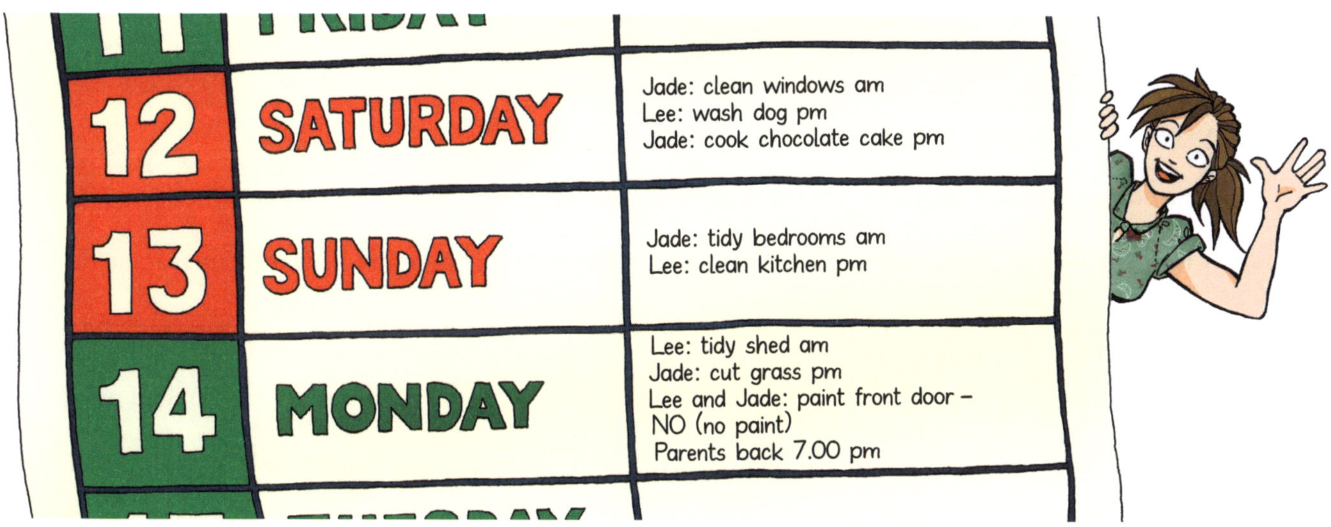

1. By Saturday afternoon, Jade will have cleaned all the windows ______.
2. By Saturday evening, ______ the dog.
3. By then, Jade ______.
4. By Sunday afternoon, ______.
5. ______ by Sunday evening.
6. By Monday afternoon, Lee ______.
7. Before their parents come back on Monday evening, ______.
8. ______ because they don't have any paint.

9 Pair words crossword

→ G18

Complete the crossword with things that are usually described as ***A pair of …*** *You must work it out from the letters that are already in the puzzle. Clue: They are all things you can wear.*

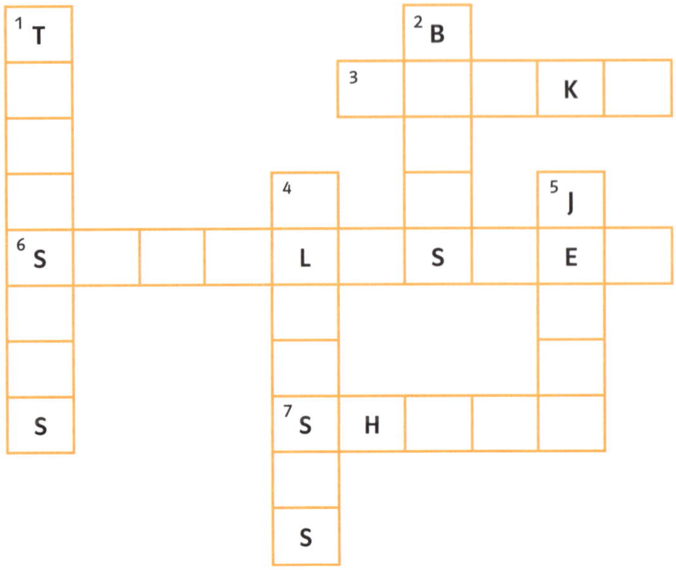

10 Mixed bag: The shoemaker

Read the joke and underline the best word from each pair to complete it.

The shoemaker

John came out of (the/–) prison after ten years. He was walking along (the/a) street, enjoying feeling free again, when he saw (the/a) shoemaker's shop. He remembered that just before he went to prison he had taken (a pair of/a pair) old brown shoes into this shop. Then he remembered that he was wearing (the/–) same coat he wore on the day he went to prison. He felt in (the/–) pocket and found (–/a) small piece of paper. It was (the/a) ticket the shoemaker had given him all those years ago. "Well," he thought, "I can't lose anything by asking if they're still there after all this time." He opened (the/–) door of the shop and went in. He (became/felt) a little strange as he walked up to the shoemaker. "Excuse me," he said. "This is going to (sound/be) crazy, but I brought (a pair of/a pair) shoes to you ten years ago to mend. They're not still here, are they?" Then he gave the ticket to the shoemaker. It (seemed/felt) certain that the shoemaker was going to say that he had thrown them away years ago, but he looked at the ticket, stood up and went into (the/–) back of his shop. After (a/–) few minutes he came back out to (the/–) front of the shop again. "(I'll have/I've) finished them by next Friday," he said.

Unit 5 Media messages

1 Media sentences

→ G19

Connect the words and phrases to make sentences in the passive form.

The Harry Potter books	is advertised	at newsagents all over the country.
Italian, French and German	is filmed	by people of all ages.
The magazine 'Shout'	is played	by the actor Joseph Harper.
The band's new album	are read	by thousands of people every day.
The advertisements	is sold	in a large school in Manchester.
The role of the hero	are spoken	in Switzerland.
The soap	are watched	on TV and radio.

2 A magazine article

→ G19

Read the magazine article and put the verbs into the correct form. Use simple present, simple past or present perfect passive forms.

Hollywood comes to town!

Most of the time, the quiet town of Kilgowan, on the West coast of Scotland, ____________________ (know) for its quiet life and its beautiful sea views. But in the last few weeks, the town ____________________ (turn) into an exciting world of Hollywood magic and famous actors. Many scenes from the new teenage vampire film *Last Sunset* ____________________ (film) there in the last three weeks. Many buildings in Kilgowan ____________________ (use) for the filming, including the famous Kilgowan castle. One of the stars of the film, 17-year-old Alex Stewart, was born in the town. Alex, who plays the part of a good-looking young vampire, ____________________ (cast) from hundreds of other young actors for the role. Alex ____________________ (ask) how he felt to be back in Kilgowan. "It's great to be here! I ____________________ (fly) in last week from Los Angeles, where the first part of the film ____________________ (set). I'm surprised that my home town ____________________ (choose) for the Scottish scenes of the film."

3 Making *Last Sunset*

→ G19

Underline the correct active or passive form of the verb.

1. Alex (cast/was cast) as the hero of the movie.
2. The director (told/was told) the actors to be at the studio by 9.00.
3. The film (has advertised/has been advertised) on television.
4. The script (wrote/was written) by Helena Orlando.
5. The casting director (chose/was chosen) Alex from hundreds of other actors.
6. The castle (has used/has been used) in several other films.
7. People in the town (asked/were asked) not to come near the castle during the filming.
8. Fans (asked/were asked) Alex to sign copies of the book *Last Sunset*.

4 From active to passive

→ G20

a) *Use a passive form to rewrite the sentences. Do not add the by-agent in these sentences.*

1. Someone has sent Alex a contract to sign. Alex has been sent a contract to sign.
2. Somebody has stolen my mobile phone. ______
3. People know Francis Herring for his horror stories. ______
4. They told Kate to smile for the camera. ______
5. Someone built the castle in 1584. ______
6. Some people have cut down these trees. ______
7. They showed this ad on TV last month. ______

b) *Use a passive form to rewrite the sentences. This time, add the by-agent.*

1. A snake bit me in the leg. I was bitten in the leg by a snake.
2. A German photographer took this photo. ______
3. The cat has broken the glass bowl. ______
4. My mother drew that picture of me. ______
5. Henry Forster played the role of the doctor. ______
6. The gardener has planted five new trees. ______
7. A twelve-year-old girl found the lost dog. ______
8. The casting agent has chosen the actors. ______

5 Mediatek Multimedia Centre

→ G21

Mediatek, a new multimedia centre, is going to open in the town of Bridgeport soon. Look at the notes for the first few events for the centre.

February	complete building work
March	work on library area and cinema screen
April 2nd	open Multimedia Centre to the general public show *Introducing Mediatek* (free film) to public
April 12th	hold free computer course
April 25th	hold sale[1] of local paintings and photographs (give money to charity)
May 1st	Bridgeport Players perform *Romeo and Juliet*

Complete the sentences about the centre. Use future passive forms of the verbs in brackets.

1. Building work on the Multimedia centre … will be completed in February. (complete)
2. The library and the cinema screen … ______ (work on)
3. The Multimedia centre … ______ (open)
4. A free film, *Introducing Mediatek* … ______ (show)
5. A free computer course … ______ (hold)
6. Local paintings and photographs … ______ (sell)
7. All money from the sale … ______ (give)
8. *Romeo and Juliet* … ______ (perform)

6 The past perfect passive

→ G21

Complete these sentences. Use the past perfect passive form.

1. Dave wasn't sure the address on the letter was right, but unfortunately it had already been posted. (post)
2. The dog was hungry because it ______ anything to eat. (not/give)
3. If the book ______ about so much on TV, nobody would have bought it. (not/talk)
4. I couldn't see what was different about Tina until I saw that her hair ______. (cut)
5. Sally was angry because she ______ the job. (not/give)
6. Tony tried to open the door, but the lock[2] ______. (change)
7. The room was very dirty because it ______ for ages. (not/clean)
8. When we got home we noticed that the window ______. (break)

[1] sale [seɪl] – Verkauf • [2] lock [lɒk] – Schloss

7 A letter from France

→ G22

Carla is writing to her sister about her new modelling career.
Read her e-mail and complete the sentences below.
Use passive forms.

From: carla@funmail.co.uk
To: alice@funmail.co.uk — Address book
Subject: Hello from Paris

Hi Alice!

So here I am in my five star hotel room with a view of the Eiffel Tower! I can't believe that they chose me to be a model, instead of all those other girls. It's so exciting! Anyway, they flew me into Paris on Monday morning. The flight was OK, but they hadn't told me to go to Terminal Two, so I went to the wrong terminal at first.

On Tuesday, a taxi took me to the studio and they gave me some great clothes to wear. They are going to use the photographs in a fashion magazine next month. They have photographed me so many times already this week that I can hear the noise of the camera in my head when I try to go to sleep! Tomorrow, they will show me how to walk in the shoes they gave me. It's going to be hard work, I think, but I'm sure they will look after me well while I'm here.

I'm really enjoying myself here, but I'm also looking forward to seeing you again! I'll send you another e-mail next week.

Lots of love
Carla

1. Carla can't believe that she ______________________ to be a model, instead of all those other girls.
2. She ______________________ into Paris on Monday morning.
3. Carla ______________________ to go to Terminal Two.
4. She ______________________ to the studio by taxi.
5. She ______________________ some great clothes to wear.
6. The photographs ______________________ in a fashion magazine next month.
7. Carla ______________________ so many times she can hear the noise of the camera in her head.
8. Tomorrow she ______________________ how to walk in the shoes she's been given.
9. She ______________________ after well while she is in Paris.
10. Carla's sister Alice ______________________ another e-mail next week.

8 A cartoon: The History lesson

9 Mixed bag: A pirate story

Change these sentences from the active to the passive form.

1. Sara Philips wrote the book *The Pirate's Daughter* in 2009.

   The book *The Pirate's Daughter* ______________________ in 2009 by Sara Philips.

2. Someone gave Sara Philips a prize for the best children's book of the year.

   Sara Philips ______________________ a prize for the best children's book of the year.

3. Sara says that nobody had ever written a book quite like this before.

   Sara says that a book like this ______________________ before.

4. They have just turned it into a film.

   It ______________________ into a film.

5. Mark Harrison directed the film.

   The film ______________________ Mark Harrison.

6. They will show the film in cinemas across the world early next year.

   The film ______________________ in cinemas across the world early next year.

7. Everybody thinks that a lot of people will watch it.

   Everybody thinks that it ______________________.

8. Sara Philips will finish her new book, *Island of Pirates*, next autumn.

   Sara Philips' new book, *Island of Pirates*, ______________________ next autumn.

Unit 6 Time to travel

1 What did Mina say?

→ G23, G24

Read the text about Mina and use it to write what she said in direct speech. Put in the verbs in the correct tense.

Mina said that it was raining heavily and she was cold and wet. She said she felt terrible. Her car had broken down so she couldn't drive to the office. She was going to be late for work.

"It ______ heavily and I ______ cold and wet. I ______ terrible. My car ______ down, so I ______ drive to the office. I ______ late for work!"

2 What did Karl say?

→ G24

Now look at what Karl said. Complete the missing words in the text. Think carefully about which tense to use.

Karl said he ______ on the beach. He ______ hot but comfortable. He said that he ______ the sea and he ______ a good book to read. He said he ______ it at the airport. He said he ______ a swim and he ______ great.

3 Match the phrases

→ G24

Match the sentences in direct speech with the reported sentences.

1. "I watch TV."
2. "I'm watching TV."
3. "I watched TV."
4. "I've been watching TV."
5. "I can watch TV."
6. "I'll watch TV."
7. "I have to watch TV."

a) He said he had to watch TV.
b) He said he watched TV.
c) He said he was watching TV.
d) He said he could watch TV.
e) He said he would watch TV.
f) He said he had watched TV.
g) He said he had been watching TV.

4 What did they actually say?

→ G25

Write what the speakers said in direct speech.

1. She told me she was going to the travel agency that day. "I'm going to the travel agency today."
2. They said they would be in New York the next day.

   ____.
3. He said that he would be back home the following week.

   ____.
4. They said that they had been to the airport that morning.

   ____.
5. She said that she had got my e-mail about the flight the day before.

   ____.
6. She told me that her cousins were coming to stay there the following month.

   ____.

5 Jacob's letter

→ G26

Read Jacob's letter to Faisal. Then complete the missing words in the conversation between Faisal and Hamid.

Hello Faisal!
I hope you and Hamid are well. Been really busy this week — so much homework!!! I had an important Maths exam on Friday, but it went OK, I think.
Thanks for your letter! Yes, of course you can stay with us next weekend. Tell me what time your coach arrives — we can pick you up from the coach station.
Looking forward to next weekend Jacob

Faisal: I've just got a letter from Jacob.

Hamid: That's great. What does he say?

Faisal: He says he ______________ we are well. He writes that he ______________ busy with homework this week. He says he ______________ an important Maths exam on Friday but he thinks it ______________ OK.

Hamid: What does he say about next weekend? Did he get our letter?

Faisal: He thanks us for the letter and he says we ______________ stay with him next weekend.

Hamid: Great! Anything else?

Faisal: Yes, he says we should tell him what time our coach ______________ so he ______________ from the coach station.

6 Karin's exam

→ G27

Karin has just had a speaking exam at school. The other students want to know about the kind of questions the teacher is going to ask them. Look at the teacher's list of questions, then complete the conversation between Karin and her classmates.

1. Where do you live?
2. Do you have any brothers or sisters?
3. Where were you born?
4. Have you ever been abroad?
5. Can you play any musical instruments?
6. Are you going to play in the school concert at the end of term?

"The speaking exam was easy! First she asked me where I lived and ______ any brothers or sisters. After that she asked me ______. Then she asked me ______ abroad. I said that I had been to Canada. After that she asked me ______ any musical instruments. I told her that I could play the piano and she asked me ______ in the school concert at the end of term. That's all! You'll be fine!"

7 Indirect commands

→ G28

Choose a verb from the box to rewrite each sentence. More than one verb can be correct.

advise, allow, ask, order, ~~invite~~, remind, warn

1. "Why don't you come round to my house this evening?"
   He invited me to go round to his house.
2. "Be careful! The paint is wet! Don't touch it!"
   He ______ the wet paint.
3. "Don't forget to turn out the lights when you leave."
   He ______ out the lights.
4. "If I were you, I'd go to bed now."
   He ______ to bed.
5. "Drop the gun right now!"
   He ______ the gun immediately.
6. "When you arrive, can you phone me please?"
   He ______ him when I arrived.
7. "You can borrow my bike if you like."
   He ______ his bike.

8 Harry's trip

→ G28

Harry is going on his first trip away from home and his mother has spoken to him before he leaves. Read Harry's note to Jack, then try to guess what his mother's words were and complete the dialogue.

Hi Jack!
I'm off tomorrow! It's very exciting to go away on my own. But my mother has been telling me what to do all week. I'll tell you what she said just now, over dinner.
She advised me to take good shoes with me. Then she warned me to be careful of the water.
Then she reminded me to take suntan cream[1]. After that she ordered me to phone home every day.
Then she told me not to go swimming on my own. And then she warned me about pickpockets[2].
And finally, she told me to bring back something for my grandmother! That's seven things, in just a few minutes! She's driving me crazy!
Anyway, I'll e-mail you when I'm away. Just don't give me any advice!
Harry

[1] suntan cream ['sʌntæn kriːm] – Sonnencreme • [2] pickpocket ['pɪkpɒkɪt] – Taschendieb

Harry's Mother: 1. "You should take good shoes with you!"

Harry: Yes, Mum, I've already packed them, see?

Harry's Mother: 2. ______________________________.

Harry: OK, OK, I'll only drink bottled water.

Harry's Mother: 3. ______________________________.

Harry: Don't worry! I never forget to take suntan cream.

Harry's Mother: 4. ______________________________.

Harry: Every day! I'll phone you two or three times a week. That's enough.

Harry's Mother: 5. ______________________________.

Harry: No problem. I don't like swimming.

Harry's Mother: 6. ______________________________.

Harry: Yes, yes, I'll be very careful about pickpockets.

Harry's Mother: 7. ______________________________.

Harry: OK. I'll bring her some sweets. She loves sweets.

9 A cartoon: A new hairstyle

10 Mixed bag: The penguin[1]

Underline the correct words from each pair to complete this joke.

The Penguin

One day a woman was working outside in her garden when a car drove up and stopped just outside her house. The driver opened the window and the woman was surprised to see a small penguin sitting on the back seat. The woman asked the driver why (had he/he had) a penguin in his car. The driver explained that he (found/had found) the penguin (a few hours earlier/a few hours ago). The penguin (looks/had looked) sad, so the man had put it into his car. The driver told the woman that he (has tried/was trying) to think of what to do with the penguin. He asked her (if she had/whether had she) any ideas. The woman thought for a moment and then told the man that (there is/there was) a zoo not far from (here/there). She suggested that the driver take the penguin there. The man thanked the woman and drove away. (The next day/Tomorrow), the woman saw the same car pull up outside her house again. She was surprised to see that the penguin was still sitting in the back of the man's car. "What happened?" asked the woman. "I thought you were taking him to the zoo." "I did, thanks!" answered the man. "He loved it, so (I'm taking/I was taking) him to the cinema (today/on that day)."

[1] **penguin** ['peŋgwɪn] – Pinguin

Unit 1 New York City

1 What's the reason?

→ G1

Match the two parts of the mini-dialogues.

1. Your eyes are red. What have you been doing?
2. You're very wet. What have you been up to?
3. You've got something red on the end of your nose. What have you been doing?
4. You poor thing! You look so tired.
5. Why are you two kids looking so sad?
6. You are looking very happy. What's been going on?
7. Look at you! You're all covered with flour!

a) I've been painting a picture. It must be paint.
b) I've been waiting for a bus in the rain.
c) Yes, I've been making a cake.
d) I've been watching a sad movie.
e) Yes, I know. I haven't been sleeping very well recently.
f) I've been talking to Joe. He just asked me out.
g) It's been snowing all morning and we haven't been able to go out and play in it.

2 *For* and *since*

→ G2

a) *Put these expressions into the correct table.*

~~2011~~ ~~a long time~~ ages the summer he was a child a few days her last birthday I was at school last spring last Wednesday the last two months three weeks years and years yesterday

For	Since
a long time	2011

b) *Now underline the correct word to complete these grammar rules.*

1. We use (for/since) when we are talking about a point in time when an action began.
2. We use (for/since) when we are talking about the period of time an action has been going on.

Present Perfect Progressive
vgl. Grammar p. 39 ff.

3 Meet Kora

→ G2

Read the radio interview and underline the right word.

Interviewer: Kora is from New York but she was born in Poland. Kora, how long have you been living in the States?

Kora: Well, I came over here when I was twelve years old, so I've been living here (1) (for/since) then.

Interviewer: Do you think of yourself as a Pole or a New Yorker?

Kora: Well, maybe both. (2) (For/Since) hundreds of years New York has been a place where new faces from different cultures arrive and make a new life. I've been living here (3) (for/since) such a long time now that it feels like home.

Interviewer: Where in New York do you live, Kora?

Kora: In Brooklyn. I've been living in my apartment (4) (for/since) five years now. The neighbourhood has been slowly changing ever (5) (for/since) I first moved in. There are more restaurants, more bars and more coffee shops now. It's a cool place to live.

Interviewer: Have more people been finding jobs (6) (for/since) the new businesses started coming into the area?

Kora: Yes! In fact, I got a job in a new Polish restaurant. I've been working there now (7) (for/since) December. I really enjoy it and the food is great!

Interviewer: I'll have to come in and try it! I've been planning to try Polish food (8) (for/since) years! Thanks for coming in to talk to us today, Kora! It's been really interesting.

4 How long have you been doing it?

→ G1, G2

*Make questions with **How long** + the present perfect progressive form.*

1. How long/go to/your school? ____________________
2. How long/sit in/that chair? ____________________
3. How long/live in/your home? ____________________
4. How long/learn/English? ____________________
5. How long/do/this exercise? ____________________

5 A cartoon: A new waiter

Grammar S. 47

6 I'd been waiting for hours

→ G3

Complete the sentences with the past perfect progressive form of the verbs in the boxes.

talk | not rain | ~~drive~~ | sunbathe | live | think | work | wait

1. Gus had been driving for four hours and the lights from the other cars were starting to give him a headache.
2. John was really tired because he ______ at his computer all night.
3. We ______ in the apartment for a very long time before we noticed a strange smell in the bathroom.
4. I arrived at the diner late, and Karen was angry because she ______ for me for ages.
5. I was really surprised to hear that Pete had left the country because I ______ to him on the phone only the week before.
6. It ______ long before the cat ran back inside, wet through.
7. She ______ about buying a new computer for a long time, but she didn't have enough money.
8. Phillip was looking very happy and relaxed because he ______ on the beach all morning.

7 Good to see you well!

→ G4

Choose a verb and an adjective from each box to complete the dialogue. Use each word only once.

called • find • makes • see • try

hard • nervous • well • safer • stupid

Colleen: Hi James! How are you doing? It's good to ______________ (verb) you ______________ (adjective) after your skydiving accident.

James: Thanks, I'm feeling much better now. I still ______________ (verb) it ______________ (adjective) to walk on my leg again now but my arm doesn't hurt any more.

Colleen: That's good. That kind of sport ______________ (verb) me ______________ (adjective). I'd have been too afraid to jump out a plane like that. I'm always scared of high places.

James: My mum ______________ (verb) me ______________ (adjective) for even trying it and, of course, after the accident she just said 'I told you so!' But skydiving isn't that dangerous, really.

Colleen: But you don't want to do it again, do you?

James: No, maybe not. I think I'll ______________ (verb) something ______________ (adjective) next time!

Colleen: Look after yourself, James!

8 Adjective or adverb?

→ G5

Underline the correct word to complete each sentence.

1. I felt like a (complete/completely) idiot when I got lost on the subway.
2. The food in the diner was (pretty/prettily) good, but I'd eaten better.
3. It was (real/really) interesting to see so many different cultures in New York.
4. We wanted to visit Alaska but the (extreme/extremely) weather made travel too difficult.
5. When I looked around for Alice in Central Park she had (complete/completely) disappeared.
6. The view from the top of the skyscraper was (quiet/quite) amazing.
7. Carmen is (amazing/amazingly) good at learning languages. She didn't speak English when she arrived in New York last year, and now it's very good.
8. I've chatted with people from the States on the Internet but never in (real/really) life.

9 All about New York City

→ G6

Put the phrases in the right order to complete these sentences.

1. Visitors to New York … (the street numbers/find it difficult/often/to understand)

____

2. In the winter … (in Central Park/always/to skate/there is/a big place)

____

3. Every year … (there is/for Saint Patrick's Day/in March/a big festival)

____

4. In the summer … (leave/for a few weeks/lots of New Yorkers/the hot city)

____

5. There are many … (held/all through the year/art exhibitions/in the city)

____

6. In the spring … (to see/the trees in flower/into the gardens/come/many tourists)

____

10 Mixed bag: In the museum

Underline the correct word or phrase from each pair to complete the joke.

Some tourists were visiting the American Museum of Natural History in New York. One of the group (has been standing/had been standing) in front of one of the dinosaurs (for/since) a while, looking at the sign and looking worried. After a few minutes, he decided to ask the museum assistant a question. "Excuse me, could you help me, please? I was wondering about the date of this dinosaur right here. Could you tell me how old these dinosaurs are?" The museum assistant replied right away, "I'm glad you (find/keep) the dinosaurs (interesting/interestingly), sir. They're three million and twelve years, five months and two weeks old." "That's (quite/very) amazing! I'd never have imagined they were so old," said the visitor. "But how on earth do you know the date so exactly?" The assistant answered, "Well, when I started work here, I asked the same question. I was told that the dinosaurs were three million years old, and (I've been/I'd been) working here (for/since) twelve years, five months and two weeks."

Unit 2 Go, Bears, go!

1 Giving advice

→ G7

*Give some advice about these situations. Use **should/shouldn't** + the perfect infinitive.*

1. I ate a whole box of chocolate. I feel sick now.

   You shouldn't have eaten so much chocolate.

2. I know you told me not to tell Kate your secret but I forgot. Sorry!

   ____

3. Sorry I'm late! I stopped on the way to school to buy a magazine.

   ____

4. I didn't do my homework because I couldn't remember which exercise the teacher told us to do.

   ____

5. I left my dad's mobile phone on the bus. He's going to be angry with me.

   ____

6. I know you told me not to watch that film, but I watched it anyway. It was terrible. What a waste of time!

   ____

7. I got really bad marks in my Maths test last week. My mum's not very happy with me.

   ____

2 Good listeners

→ G7

Match the two parts of the mini-dialogues. Draw lines to the right answers.

1. "I wanted to relax so I ran a bath – but I forgot to put hot water in it."
2. "When I got back home I noticed that I'd been wearing one blue sock and one black one."
3. "I worked for two whole days without sleeping last week."
4. "I did really well in my final exam last week."
5. "I broke my leg a few years ago."
6. "Last week my sister borrowed my phone, and then she lost it."

a) "Oh dear. That must have been painful."
b) "You must have been really happy about that!"
c) "You poor thing! You must have been very tired."
d) "Oh no! That must have been very embarrassing for you!"
e) "You must have felt really angry with her."
f) "Oh dear! That must have been very cold!"

3 You needn't have done that!

→ G7

*Use **need** + **not** + the perfect infinitive to make sentences about these situations. Use the words in brackets.*

1. There's a dishwasher in the kitchen, you know. (you/do all the washing up)
   You needn't have done all the washing up.
2. Thank you for all the delicious food you cooked for us last Sunday. (you/go to all that trouble)
   ____
3. I got a phone call from Phil this morning. (I/send him that e-mail)
   ____
4. That list of verbs wasn't in the test. (we/learn them by heart)
   ____
5. Their old phone was perfectly OK. (they/buy a new one)
   ____
6. It's been raining all afternoon. (I/water the plants this morning)
   ____

4 Trouble at school

→ G7

Read Karin's e-mail to her cousin and underline the correct modal auxiliaries.

From: karin@funmail.co.uk
To: tina@funmail.co.uk
Subject: Trouble at school

Address book

Hi Tina!

Did I mention in my last e-mail that there's a big dance at school this coming weekend? I think I (can't/might/needn't) have done. Anyway, I was talking to Danni after French class today and I asked her what she was going to wear to the dance. Well, I really (mustn't/might not/shouldn't) have said anything. I knew I (can/must/should) have said the wrong thing because she just went really quiet and I noticed her eyes were red. It looked like she (should/can/might) have been crying earlier. So, it turns out that Amy and Danni had a big argument this morning about a boy. Amy invited Paul from the volleyball team to the dance and he agreed. The problem was that Paul had already asked Danni to go with him. Amy (can't/mustn't/shouldn't) have known about it before, because it had only happened the night before. Paul really (might not/can't/shouldn't) have said 'yes' to Amy! It's all very silly, really, and none of this (can/could/should) have happened. The thing is, I know Paul quite well because he's in my brother's class, and I know that you can't count on him. If I had told Danni what Paul was really like, she and Amy (must not/cannot/might not) have had this horrible argument! What do you think about this? Hope to hear from you soon!

Karin

5 Where could I have left it?

→ G7

Read the dialogue and put in the missing words. Choose one of these modal auxiliaries: ***might/could/can't/must/should*** *+ the perfect infinitive of the verb in brackets.*

Dave: Hey, Sally, have you seen my phone? I can't find it anywhere.

Sally: I haven't got it. You ______________________ (leave) it at home.

Dave: No, I ______________________ (not/do). I remember looking at it on the bus.

Sally: You ______________________ (put) it down when we were eating in the diner this evening.

Dave: Oh, I don't know. I ______________________ (do), I suppose. I remember taking a photo of you when we got there. And then when the food arrived, I was so busy talking and eating that I ______________________ (forget) it. I ______________________ (be) more careful.

Sally: Don't be sad, Dave. It could still be there. Someone ______________________ (find) it and given it to the manager.

Dave: We could go back and ask them if they've seen it. Do you think the diner will still be open now?

Sally: No, it ______________________ (close) by now. It's nearly midnight. You could phone them tomorrow to see if it's there. I ______________________ (pick) up a card with the phone number on it, maybe. Hold on a moment and I'll have a look. Yes! Here you are.

Dave: Thanks, Sally! I ______________________ (think) of that!

6 The passive infinitive

→ G8

Pick the right verbs to complete these sentences. Use the passive infinitive with ***to****.*

call | finish | show | ~~offer~~ | allow | tell | give | make

1. I'd love to be offered the chance to visit the States.
2. My boss expects ______________________ 'sir', which I think is stupid.
3. I hope ______________________ to get a Saturday job next week, after my sixteenth birthday.
4. The twins are terrible! They expect ______________________ anything they want for Christmas.
5. I would like ______________________ about any changes to my hotel booking, please.
6. These cookies are horrible. They seem ______________________ of wood!
7. This work has ______________________ before the end of the week.
8. It's OK, thanks. I understand. I don't need ______________________ how to do it!

7 Lucy's Saturday job

→ G8

Lucy has just started a Saturday job in a restaurant. Look at the list of jobs she and the other workers have to finish this morning.

MEMO: Saturday am

clean floor
~~wash windows~~ – no need – did it!
cut up vegetables
take out rubbish
lay tables
put flowers on tables
polish glasses
~~write menu board~~ – done this already!

Write sentences with ***need to*** *or* ***have to*** *+ the passive infinitive about what needs to be done.*

The floor needs to be cleaned. The windows don't need to be washed.

____

____

____

____

8 He should be told!

→ G8

Use a passive form to rewrite these sentences.

1. You can buy tickets from the school secretary.
   Tickets can be bought from the school secretary.
2. Watch out! Someone might steal your bike if you leave it there.
   ____
3. I think someone should tell the teacher what's been happening.
   ____
4. Nobody should use this classroom for the next 24 hours. Someone has just painted it.
   ____
5. They might build a new swimming pool at school next year.
   ____
6. You can borrow computer games from the new library.
   ____

9 Mixed bag: Modal auxiliaries and the passive

a) *Replace the underlined modal verb with one that fits better.*

1. Thanks for picking me up! But you really can't have done, I could have taken the bus. ____________________
2. I'm sorry to hear that you were sick for two weeks. That should have been terrible! ____________________
3. Hey! You needn't have eaten that sandwich, it was mine! ____________________
4. Why didn't you tell me you had trouble with your homework? I must have helped you. ____________________

b) *Choose the correct phrase to complete each sentence.*

to be cleaned | can be found | to be finished | to be paid | could have walked | might be accepted | might have left | should have bought

1. If Dave trains hard this month, he ____________________ into the basketball team.
2. I can't find my watch anywhere, but I think I ____________________ it in the gym.
3. I only started playing football for fun. I really didn't expect ____________________ for it.
4. You forgot to close the gym door last night. Anybody ____________________ in off the street.
5. These trainers are far too big for me. I really ____________________ a smaller size.
6. Very talented young players ____________________ on the playing fields of most schools.
7. The sports centre windows are so dirty I can hardly see through them.

   They ought ____________________.
8. The work on the new sports stadium ought ____________________ before the end of the year.

10 A cartoon: Chicken soup

Unit 3 Out West

1 From coast to coast

→ G9

Lazlo has recently returned to his home in Budapest after a holiday of a lifetime in the States. Read the magazine article and complete the text with the missing subjects.

a) Being able to speak naturally to people in English
b) Looking out of the window
c) Getting from the East coast to the West coast
d) Travelling across the States
e) Reading and writing in English
f) Taking pictures from a moving train
g) Sitting for hours talking with a stranger

"This summer I decided to make a dream of mine come true – to travel from New York to San Francisco without flying. ______________________ by train takes a lot longer than flying, of course, but it's been a good way to see more of the country. ______________________ and seeing the world go by means that you don't have the typical tourist's view of the United States.

I didn't speak English very well before my trip. ______________________ wasn't really a problem for me, but speaking and listening used to be much harder. I've had lots of practice chatting to American people as I was travelling. ______________________ is an excellent way to turn a stranger into a friend. I've learnt a lot about how to make conversation, too. ______________________ is a skill I'll always be proud of in later life. I took some photographs as I was travelling along, but none of them came out very well, unfortunately! ______________________ is not very easy.

If you have plenty of time for your trip, I'd really recommend this way of getting around, but it's probably not for you if you only have a week or so. I didn't need to hurry, so I took my time. ______________________ took me just over a month, but I really feel as though I know the country quite well now!"

2 Travelling on Route 66

→ G9

Rewrite these sentences with a gerund form.

1. It has always been my dream to travel on Route 66.
   Travelling on Route 66 has always been my dream.
2. A great way to get to know the country is to drive across the States.
   ____
3. The best way to learn the language is to spend time with real American people.
   ____
4. The thing I love about Florida is to be able to swim in the sea for six months of the year.
   ____
5. An important part of learning English is to know how to make polite conversation.
   ____
6. The scariest part of my trip was when I lost my passport on the train.
   ____

3 Rodeo!

→ G9

Jake has written a postcard home about his weekend. Complete the gaps with gerund forms of these verbs.

see take hurt hang kick go do watch fall

Hi everyone!

You'll never guess what I've been doing this weekend. Uncle Jim took Holly and me along to see a rodeo! At first Holly said she didn't want to go, because she says she doesn't like ______________ dangerous sports, but we managed to get her to change her mind. The rodeo stars were amazing. They get on the horse and right away it starts ______________ and ______________ completely crazy. All the time, the men have to keep ______________ on. I can't imagine ______________ it myself. The rodeo stars really risk ______________ themselves badly if they fall. The horses throw off nearly everyone in the end, but the men don't seem to mind ______________ off. I enjoyed ______________ lots of photos of my first ever rodeo, and Holly said she wouldn't have missed ______________ it for anything! I'll send some photographs so you can see for yourself. It was great! I'll e-mail again later this week.

Jake

4 Do you like the music playing on the radio?

→ G10

*Rewrite these sentences. Use the object + **-ing** construction.*

1. You always interrupt me. I'm sick of it!

   I'm sick of you always interrupting me!

2. My neighbour's dog barks every night. I'm getting fed up about it.

   I'm getting fed up about ______.

3. When people tell me what to do, I don't like it.

   I don't like ______.

4. Jane's coming back home again. I'm looking forward to it.

   I'm looking forward to ______.

5. Are you worried? Your computer's making that funny noise again.

   Are you worried about ______?

6. My little sister borrows all my things. I'm used to it.

   I'm used to ______.

7. My cousins are visiting me tomorrow. I'm excited about it.

   I'm excited about ______.

5 Polite requests

→ G10

*Choose a verb and an object from the boxes to complete the sentences. Use the **-ing** form of the verbs.*

Object	Verb
my cousin, the children, the dog, the elevator, ~~me~~, the rain	come down, be, come to stay, not work, ~~open~~, shout

1. Would you mind me opening the window for a moment?
2. I don't mind ______ here, but I wish he'd keep quiet.
3. I didn't really mind ______ because they were only having fun.
4. I wouldn't mind ______ if there were only a few steps.
5. Adam didn't mind ______ on his head.
6. Would you mind ______ for the weekend?

6 Joshua Tree National Park

→ G11

Read the article about the park and fill in the gaps with the passive forms given.

was created | are asked | will be built | was made | have been written | to be enjoyed | are not allowed | is visited

Joshua Tree National Monument ______________________ in 1936 and ______________________ into a national park in 1994. Every year it ______________________ by more than a million people, and the number of visitors will probably go up in the coming years. Guide books for hikers ______________________ and five new information centers ______________________ this year. Many parts of the park are open ______________________ freely, but making fires and sleeping in the park ______________________ outside the official campsites. Tourists ______________________ to follow these rules.

7 From active to passive

→ G12

Use passive forms to rewrite these sentences.

1. They are building a new shopping mall next to our school.

   ____

2. When I saw the building, they were cleaning part of it.

   ____

3. They were filming a movie at the park during our visit.

   ____

4. On the news we saw a helicopter rescuing a man.

   ____

8 A cartoon: Bad dog!

9 In the right order

→ G13

Put the words and phrases in the correct order to make sentences in the passive form.

1. the members/The statue/was/paid for/by/of the City Theatre

   The statue ____________________.

2. large groups of people/being/by/don't like/looked at/I

   I ____________________.

3. by/Mike/I/let down/feel/badly

   I ____________________.

4. has been/this century/five different/countries/fought over/by/The island

   The island ____________________.

5. in the newspapers/are used to/Celebrities/written about/being

   Celebrities ____________________.

10 Mixed bag: Visiting Phoenix

Rob is telling his mother about his visit to his uncle. Put in the missing words in this phone conversation.

Mum: It's good to hear from you, Rob. I was worried about you ____________ all by yourself!

Rob: Don't worry, Mum! I'm ____________ to travelling on my own. I've done it lots of times. If I feel like ____________ to sleep on the flight, nobody wakes me up by talking to me.

Mum: Well, OK, then. What time did you get there? Did you have any problems ____________ from the airport to Uncle Joe's house?

Rob: No, none at all. I got to Phoenix Arizona just before twelve, and Uncle Joe met us at the airport. I'm ____________ looked after really well here. Joe is crazy about ____________ on the barbeque and he's made some amazing meals.

Mum: Oh yes, I know! Cooking has always been one of Joe's favourite things. Is Joe's swimming pool finished yet? He said it was ____________ built when I e-mailed him last month.

Rob: Yes! It's great. It ____________ finished a couple of weeks ago. There are still a few small things to ____________ done to the garden around the pool, but the pool itself is great. I love ____________ first thing every morning. I've ____________ treated as though I've been staying in a four star hotel these last few days. You should have come out too, Mum!

Unit 4 Extreme action

1 A postcard home

→ G14

Mike is on a hiking trip in the mountains. Read his postcard and underline the correct verb form.

Hi Mum and Dad!

I know you made me (promise/to promise) to phone home every day before you let me (come/to come) on this trip, but the phone didn't work in the mountains, so I couldn't (get/to get) through. Sorry! But it's been fun and nothing bad has happened to us, so you can (stop/to stop) worrying! On the very first day, we came to a big river. The only way we could (cross/to cross) over the river was (jump/to jump) over it and guess what? I fell in and got really wet! The first evening we knew we shouldn't (be/to be) hiking at night, so we decided (stop/to stop). We needed (get/to get) the tent up quickly before it was too dark (see/to see) anything. It was the first time we'd ever put up the tent, but I must (say/to say), you learn new skills quickly when you need to!

Anyway, I'll phone you soon, love from Mike

2 Stay on the paths!

→ G14

A park ranger is talking to a group of visitors. Put the words in the right order to fill the gaps with the missing phrases.

not • to • take • ask • you

~~listen • all • you • want • to~~

anyone • get • don't • to • want

all • to • need • stay • you

you • warn • not • pick • to

not • tell • get • to • you

"I want you all to listen carefully, please! First of all, I have to ______ any of the plants that you see on your way. Some of them are very poisonous. We may get the chance to see some interesting animals such as eagles or even bears. Although it's very exciting to see these amazing animals, we ______ safe and to stay on the paths with the group at all times. If we do see a bear, I'm sure I don't have to ______ too close or to make any loud noises. I have to ______ any strong-smelling food with you into the park. We have had situations where people have been attacked by bears for food and we really ______ hurt today!"

3 Jumbled sentences

→ G14

Put the words and phrases in the correct order to make sentences.

1. Sam • so well • the competition • Nobody • to do • expected • in

   Nobody ______________________________.

2. these books • want • to put • Where • do • me • you

   Where ______________________________?

3. me • to climb • there • expect • Do • up • you

   Do ______________________________?

4. you • to know • I am • pleased • to win • this award • how • I want

   I want ______________________________.

5. prefer • to e-mail you • or to phone you • you • me • Would

   Would ______________________________?

6. to take • us • clothes • The instructors • warm • advised

   The instructors ______________________________.

4 Lizzie's trip

→ G14

Lizzie is planning to go hiking in Colorado. There are lots of things she wants to find out:

~~Which shoes should I take with me?~~
Should I take a camera with me or not?
What kind of bag should I take with me?
How much money should I take with me?
What time of year should I go?
Where could I buy a good map of the area?
Who can I ask about the best routes?

Use an infinitive form to complete these sentences.

1. She doesn't know which shoes to take with her.
2. She isn't sure whether ______________________________
3. She wonders what ______________________________
4. She has no idea how much ______________________________
5. She isn't sure what ______________________________
6. She wonders where ______________________________
7. She doesn't know who ______________________________

5 A 75th birthday party

→ G14

Olivia is telling Matt about her weekend. Choose a phrase from the first box and a verb from the second box to complete the gaps in the dialogue.

the best person • the best way • the first • ~~the most interesting way~~ • the last • the youngest • the oldest woman in the country • the next

to arrive • to do • to get • to go • to have • to find out • ~~to spend~~ • to make

Matt: Did you have a good weekend?

Olivia: Not bad. It was my great aunt's 75th birthday and I had to go to her birthday party.

Matt: Really? How did it go?

Olivia: It was OK, I guess. It wasn't the most interesting way to spend Saturday night, but I couldn't really say no when Mum asked. Mum made us get there early. We were ______________ there and we helped to get everything ready.

Matt: Yes, your mum is ______________ around when you need to organise things.

Olivia: You mean she always tells people what to do? Yes, she does! Then my brother and his wife were ______________ there.

Matt: Your brother's married? I had no idea) But I'm always ______________ about that kind of thing. Were there lots of people there?

Olivia: Yes, about 25 people. I was ______________ to the party, because most of my great aunt's friends are even older than she is. One of her friends, who is called Jennifer, is 85 and she's ______________ bungee jumping for charity!

Matt: Really? That's great! That's ______________ money. I'd love to do that myself!

6 A cartoon: It never stops raining in Seattle

7 Find the mistakes

→ G15

Underline the grammatical mistakes in these sentences. Then write down the correct version.

1. I'd like be able to drive because I hate have to walk to school in the rain.

   ____

2. Thanks for the offer help, but I think I prefer to doing it myself.

   ____

3. It's started rain again, so our idea of to go to the beach will have to wait until tomorrow.

   ____

4. I like watching other people to do dangerous things, but I'm not interested in to do them myself.

   ____

5. I'm used to get up early, but now the days have started get so short it's harder for me.

   ____

6. My brother loves to watching TV in the evening, but I prefer to reading.

   ____

8 Gerund or infinitive?

→ G15

Put in the correct gerund or infinitve form of the verbs in brackets to complete the sentences.

1. If Kate's not answering her phone, you could try ______________ her mobile number. (call)
2. We wanted to get home before dark, which meant ______________ for six hours without a break after lunch. (walk)
3. We didn't want to go up the mountain without any water, so we stopped ______________ a bottle on the way. (buy)
4. I asked Jim to slow down a little because he was walking too quickly for me, but he just went on ______________ up the hill as fast as ever. (climb)
5. I tried ______________ over the river, but I didn't jump far enough so I got wet. (jump)
6. Although she didn't learn to ski until she was 13, Lisa Mitchell later went on ______________ the Under 18's skiing medal. (win)
7. I'm glad it's stopped ______________ at last! Now we can go out. (rain)
8. I didn't mean ______________ the compass! It just fell out of my hand. (break)

X

9 Mixed bag: Camp tales

Tom and Ben are on a hiking trip. Choose the right words or phrases to complete the dialogue.

Tom: Today has been a great day hiking! I'll never forget ____________ **1** down on the world from the top of the mountain.

Ben: No, nor me. It felt as though we were the first people ____________ **2** it!

Tom: I wonder ____________ **3** people have been all the way to the top. I'm looking forward ____________ **4** my brother about it. I meant ____________ **5** a photograph when we were up there, but I forgot ____________ **6** a camera.

Ben: My feet are beginning ____________ **7** now. Do you think we should ____________ **8** on walking or stop ____________ **9** our camp now?

Tom: I'd like to stop ____________ **10** now, I think. But I'm not sure ____________ **11** this would be a good place to camp or not. What do you think?

Ben: Yes, it looks OK. The place under the trees looks like the best place ____________ **12** up our tents. It's flat and dry. Would you like me to help you put up the tent or shall I ____________ **13** and try ____________ **14** some wood for a fire?

Tom: Would you mind ____________ **15** me with the tent first? I can't remember ____________ **16** to put it up.

Ben: Sure. So first we need you ____________ **17** the tent out of your bag.

Tom: *My* bag? What? I thought you were carrying it.

Ben: Oh no! Don't tell me we've forgotten ____________ **18** the tent with us!

1	a) to look	b) looking	c) look
2	a) to have climbed	b) climbed	c) climb
3	a) what	b) that	c) how many
4	a) to tell	b) telling	c) to telling
5	a) to take	b) taking	c) to taking
6	a) to bring	b) bringing	c) bring
7	a) to hurt	b) hurting	c) hurt
8	a) to keep	b) keeping	c) keep
9	a) to make	b) making	c) make
10	a) to walk	b) walking	c) to walking
11	a) whether	b) that	c) what
12	a) to put	b) putting	c) put
13	a) to go	b) going	c) go
14	a) to find	b) finding	c) find
15	a) to help	b) helping	c) help
16	a) what	b) which	c) how
17	a) to get	b) getting	c) get
18	a) to bring	b) bringing	c) bring

Unit 5 The Golden State

1 Defining or non-defining

→ G16

Are the underlined clauses defining or non-defining relative clauses? Put commas in where necessary.

	defining	non-defining
1. The film *Angels in Waiting* which stars Johnny Weiss comes out next Friday.	☐	☐
2. My youngest sister who loves everything to do with Hollywood has asked me to photograph Sunset Boulevard.	☐	☐
3. Can you lend me the DVD which you bought yesterday?	☐	☐
4. Brian Horowitz who lives near Palm Beach is a great surfer.	☐	☐
5. That's the actor who was in the movie we watched last night.	☐	☐
6. The swimsuit I bought last week which was reduced in the sale fit me perfectly.	☐	☐
7. Most of the people who we met in California were very friendly.	☐	☐
8. The San Francisco earthquake of 1906 in which around 3,000 people died is the worst in the history of the city.	☐	☐
9. I'm looking for a website which can tell me more about Drew Barrymore's life.	☐	☐
10. The best hotel we stayed in which was near Venice Beach had a great view of the sea.	☐	☐

2 Which relative pronoun?

→ G16

Underline the correct relative pronoun to complete each sentence.

1. Luke, (whose/who/which) father teaches Spanish, helped us to translate the signs.
2. The Disney store, (whose/who/which) has lots of great souvenirs, was full of people.
3. We had our first experience of surfing today, (whose/who/which) we really enjoyed, although we weren't very good at it.
4. In the evening we watched a movie about an earthquake, (whose/who/which) was a little boring.
5. Pablo, (whose/who/which) is a great friend of mine, showed us around the city.
6. We visited Sequoia National Park, in (whose/who/which) you can find the largest tree in the world.
7. Juan, (whose/who/which) job is to show tourists around the L.A. Walk of Fame, told us lots of interesting things about the stars.
8. Leonardo di Caprio, (whose/who/which) comes from Los Angeles, came to the award ceremony.

3 The Walk of Fame

→ G16

Read Sally's blog and choose the best non-defining relative clause to go into each space. Put the letters from a–h into the gaps.

So this morning we visited Hollywood! We left our car in an underground parking place. It cost about $15 for the day, ______ if you think what kind of city Los Angeles is. We looked at the city map, ______ and we set off to find the Walk of Fame. Danni, ______ brought her little camera with her. And so there we were on the Walk of Fame, ______ and took lots of pictures and looked at all the names of the stars. We bought some souvenirs and a T-shirt for Mark, ______!

Anyway, suddenly we realized there was something important going on. There was a film crew with huge cameras. They were doing an interview with the actor and director, Reese Witherspoon, ______

The filming crew doing the interview, ______ filmed the crowd too, so you can see our faces in the TV interview! Danni, ______ was so excited I thought she wouldn't stop smiling! So, anyway, our big news today is that we went to Hollywood and we got famous!

a) which we'd bought online before we came,
b) who would kill me if I went to Hollywood and didn't bring something back for him
c) which was for a national TV station,
d) which isn't too expensive really,
e) where all the names of the big stars are on the ground,
f) who was waving at the cameras,
g) who's crazy about photography,
h) who was being given a star of fame that day!

4 All about the Golden State

→ G16

Draw lines to make sentences about California.

Silicon Valley,	who were later called the forty-niners,	started the company in 1933.
Richard Nixon,	whose wine company is now the largest exporter of Californian wines,	often have snow on them all year long.
The Gold Rush in 1849 brought thousands of people,	which cover a large area of the state of California,	into the state of California in 1849.
Ernest and Julio Gallo,	who was President of the United States from 1969 to 1974,	was born in Yorba Linda, California.
Mountains,	which is where many of the world's largest technology companies have their home,	is in the San Francisco Bay area.

5 The surfing goat[1]

→ G16

Read the article about a special goat. Use non-defining relative clauses to add the missing extra information.

Dayna McGregor, who loves surfing (1), last month celebrated his birthday in an unusual way. He decided to go surfing on Grover Beach, ______ (2), and take all his friends. He also decided to take his pet goat, ______ (3), with him to the beach. Other people on the beach, ______ (4), were very surprised to see the animal there. “At first I thought it was a dog,” said Suzy Miller, “but then I saw that it was a goat, ______ (5)!” Everybody on the beach laughed when Dayna put Goatee onto a surf board, but they were amazed when the goat managed to stay on the surf board for several minutes. One of Dayna’s friends, ______ (6), filmed the surfing goat and put the video on YouTube. In only a few hours thousands of people had watched the video, ______ (7). After only a few days, Goatee was the most famous goat in the world. McGregor, ______ (8), has plans to use Goatee’s fame to do good. He told reporters he was thinking about ways to raise money for charity to buy goats in Africa, ______ (9).

1. ~~Dayna McGregor loves surfing.~~
2. Grover Beach is very popular with local surfers.
3. Dayna’s pet goat is called Goatee.
4. The other people on the beach were watching Dayna and his friends surfing.
5. It amazed Suzy when she realised the animal was a goat.
6. One of Dayna’s friends had brought a camera.
7. The video was also shown on TV.
8. Dayna MacGregor bought the goat five months ago.
9. Dayna used to live in Africa.

[1] goat [gəʊt] – Ziege

6 A cartoon: Mr Smith

7 California facts

→ G16

Choose the best non-defining relative clause (a–g) to go into each of these sentences. Make new sentences, and don't forget to use commas. Be careful, you don't need all of the relative clauses!

1. California is one of the top tourist places in the US.
2. More than 300 tons of grapes[1] are grown every year.
3. The first ever cinema in the world opened in L.A. in 1902.
4. The Beach Boys made California internationally famous.
5. In 1854 the largest piece of gold ever found was discovered in California.

a) who were a popular band in the 1960s
b) whose name comes from the enormous trees growing there
c) which was called *Tally's Electric Theater*
d) which weighed 195 pounds
e) which grow easily in California
f) who invented the first ever video tape recorder
g) which is called *The Golden State*

1. ______________________________
2. ______________________________
3. ______________________________
4. ______________________________
5. ______________________________

8 Past or present participle?

→ G17

Choose a verb from the boxes to make a past participle or present participle as an adjective.

forget | carry | build | feel | hold | post | want | breathe | enjoy | open

1. ______________ heavily, Jack ran towards the sea to meet his first wave.
2. ______________ in the nineteenth century, the house is now owned by a film producer.
3. ______________ some cold drinks, Maria walked towards the swimming pool.
4. The movie *ET*, ______________ by many, made a lot of money when it came out.
5. ______________ a little hungry, Elena and Joseph decided to look for a café.
6. The book, ______________ for years, will soon be made into a movie.
7. ______________ in 1999, the visitor centre now welcomes more than 20,000 people a year.
8. Jo was working really hard so Peter, not ______________ to interrupt, went quietly away.
9. The couple, ______________ hands as they were walking, had got married the day before.
10. The letter, ______________ last Tuesday, arrived this morning.

[1] grape [greɪp] – Weintraube

9 Mixed bag: What should you do in an earthquake?

Read the radio interview and complete the text with the correct phrases from below.

Jake: Today we're talking to Becky harper, who works for the city of Los Angeles giving advice on earthquakes. So Becky, have you ever actually been in an earthquake?

Becky: Yes, I was in the earthquake in Northridge, LA, in 1994, ______________________________. I was surprised that the earthquake, ______________________________, caused so much damage to my home. I was in the kitchen at the time and a cupboard, ______________________________, fell over and I was hit by some glasses ______________________________. Now in my home I keep everything safely in low cupboards, or ______________________________.

Jake: So what should you do if you live in an area that is likely to have earthquakes? Is there anything you can do to prepare for an earthquake?

Becky: Yes, you should prepare. You should look around your house to see if there are any objects that might fall over. And buy some flashlights[1], so if the power goes off, ______________________________, you can see enough to get out.

Jake: And how about when the earthquake is happening? What should you do then?

Becky: Well, the safest thing to do is to get under a heavy table or a bed, ______________________________. You shouldn't stand near windows because you might get hurt by ______________________________.

Jake: What if you are outside when there's an earthquake?

Becky: Try to get away from trees or power lines[2], ______________________________. Look around to find a clear open space, ______________________________.

Jake: That all sounds like good, useful advice. Thank you for talking to us today, Becky!

a) broken glass
b) falling off the shelves
c) where I was living at the time
d) where you are safer from falling trees
e) which might fall down and hurt you
f) which often happens after an earthquake
g) which only lasted for about 20 seconds
h) which was full of food
i) which will protect you from falling objects
j) safely attached to the wall

[1] flashlight [flæʃlaɪt] – Taschenlampe • [2] power line ['paʊə ˌlaɪn] – Stromkabel

Green Line 3

Lösungen

Unit 1 The world of sport

1 Talking about sport

2. is/'s going to come
3. won't rain
4. will be
5. are/'re going to watch
6. won't be
7. is/'s going to rain
8. will go
9. will/'ll be
10. are/'re going to watch

2 When does it open?

1. correct
2. not correct (I can't go shopping this afternoon because I'm watching/I'm going to watch the cricket match.)
3. not correct (Jason is meeting/is going to meet me at the swimming pool this evening.)
4. correct
5. correct
6. not correct (I'm playing/I'm going to play tennis with Joe this evening.)
7. correct
8. correct

3 Surfing course

're leaving; 's driving; 're meeting; 're watching; 're walking; 'm having; 're meeting

4 What was the reply?

1. d)
2. c)
3. a)
4. e)
5. b)

5 Sports crossword

1. who; umpire
2. who; team
3. that; helmet
4. which; cricket
5. who; skier
6. –; racket
7. who; referee

6 Sentences with *whose*

2. Jack Evans is the sports writer whose books have sold over a million copies.
3. I know a girl whose grandmother was a very famous tennis player.
4. There's a boy in my class whose parents teach skiing.
5. Who's the famous cyclist whose bike I saw outside?
6. Those are the athletes whose photos were in the newspaper.

7 *Whose* or *who's*?

1. who's
2. whose
3. who's
4. who's
5. whose
6. whose

8 Which sentence is correct?

1. a)
2. b)
3. b)
4. a)
5. a)
6. a)

9 Find the mistakes

1. I think tomorrow's match <u>is being</u> the most exciting match <u>what</u> I've ever seen.
   correct version: I think tomorrow's match **is going to be** the most exciting match **that/which**/– I've ever seen.
2. The advertisement <u>who</u> I saw said that the match <u>is beginning</u> at 2 pm.
   correct version: The advertisement **that/which**/– I saw said that the match **begins** at 2 pm.
3. I'm sure that Ellie Evans is the player <u>which</u> <u>wins</u> the most tennis matches next year.
   correct version: I'm sure that Ellie Evans is the player **who will win** the most tennis matches next year.

11 Mixed bag: The charity

are you doing; 's; 'm going to; which; 'll; going to be; 's coming; who; 'll be; 'll give; We're all meeting; 'll see

Unit 2 Once upon a time ...

1 You can and you may ...

Talking about ability: 2, 3, 6
Talking about what's allowed: 1, 4, 5, 7

2 Correct or not correct?

a)

1. not correct
2. not correct
3. correct
4. not correct
5. correct
6. not correct
7. correct
8. correct
9. not correct

b)

A. Sentence 2
B. Sentence 9
C. Sentence 1
D. Sentence 4
E. Sentence 6

3 What are they able to do?

2. haven't been able to finish
3. 'll/will be able to help
4. was able to understand
5. has been able to find
6. 'll/will be able to speak
7. wasn't able to get

GL3

4 Kim's new school

1. In my last school, students **weren't allowed to walk** on the grass or play ball games near the school buildings.
2. Now we**'re allowed to play** where we like!
3. I **wasn't allowed to wear** my favourite red shoes in my old school but my new school doesn't have any rules about shoes or other clothes.
4. We**'re allowed to wear** anything we want.
5. **Are you allowed to wear** any clothes you like in your school, too?
6. There's a swimming pool in my new school, so in summer **we're/we'll be allowed to go** swimming.

5 Similar meanings

1. d)
2. f)
3. b)
4. a)
5. e)
6. c)

6 Sam's new job

had to answer; 'll have to go; won't have to pay; haven't had to act; 've had to learn; 'll have to practise

8 A trip to London

1. will be able to/allowed to visit
2. were allowed to feed
3. been able to/allowed to go
4. 'll have to take
5. had to plan

9 The city trip

1. c)
2. e)
3. f)
4. a)
5. d)
6. b)

10 Past perfect or simple past?

2. knew; had met
3. didn't go; had visited
4. got; had (already) left
5. knew; had sent
6. arrived; had (already) gone
7. was; had been

11 Mixed bag: Trouble with Grandma

won't be able to; 'd broken; wasn't able to; needn't; mustn't; have to; don't have to; wasn't allowed to; must; had already

Unit 3 Living together

1 Parties, paint and puppies

himself; themselves; ourselves; itself; myself; itself; herself

2 Correct or not correct?

1. not correct (yourself)
2. not correct (myself)
3. correct
4. not correct (ourselves)
5. correct
6. not correct (myself)
7. not correct (ourselves)
8. correct
9. not correct (herself)

S. 14

3 A crossword

1. ourselves
2. herself
3. yourselves
4. myself
5. yourself
6. themselves
7. himself

4 Eva's e-mail

yourselves; ourselves; each other; each other; ourselves; each other; themselves; each other

S. 15

5 Broken sentences

1. c)
2. g)
3. f)
4. b)
5. a)
6. h)
7. e)
8. d)

6 What would they do?

1. had; 'd/would buy
2. were; 'd/would go
3. had; 'd/would invite
4. would (the teacher) do; saw
5. 'd/would sit; was
6. went away; would (you) have
7. knew; 'd/would mend
8. wouldn't be; knew

7 What do you wish?

2. I wish I could read Russian.
3. I wish I had a dictionary.
4. I wish he'd/she'd speak more slowly.
5. I wish I had more/enough money.
6. I wish I hadn't forgotten my Spanish.

8 The school play

1. hadn't finished; would have had to
2. had told; wouldn't have sold
3. hadn't stayed up; would have forgotten
4. hadn't been; wouldn't (nearly) have fallen

10 Mixed bag: A quiz

1. saw; I'd; me; myself
2. were; each other; ourselves; each other
3. himself; had broken; have taken; myself
4. invited; would; ourselves
5. had asked; have told; myself

Unit 4 The UK on the move

1 *The* or no article?
1. –
2. –
3. –
4. the
5. the
6. –; –
7. –
8. The

2 A conversation on a bus
the; –; a; an; a; –; the; –; a; –; the; a; the; –; a; –

3 Famous sayings
1. b)
2. e)
3. a)
4. c)
5. d)
6. f)

4 Adjectives after verbs
sounds; looked/smelled; feeling; getting; feel/seem; felt/seemed; feels/seems; gets/felt; stay

5 Adverb or adjective?
1. sadly; thin
2. late; quickly
3. happily; delicious
4. cold; fantastic
5. carefully; interesting
6. good; cheaply
7. carefully; soft
8. boring; exciting
9. nervously; calm

7 Henry's plans for the future
2. I won't have earned a million pounds.
3. I will have met a nice woman.
4. I won't have married.
5. I will have bought a car.
6. I won't have bought a house.

8 A busy weekend
2. Lee will have washed
3. will have cooked a chocolate cake
4. Jade will have tidied the bedrooms
5. Lee will have cleaned the kitchen
6. will have tidied the shed
7. Jade will have cut the grass
8. They won't have painted the front door

9 Pair words crossword
1. trousers
2. boots
3. socks
4. glasses
5. jeans
6. sunglasses
7. shoes

10 Mixed bag: The shoemaker
–; the; a; a pair of; the; the; a; the; the; felt; sound; a pair of; seemed; the; a; the; I'll have

Unit 5 Media messages

1 Media sentences
The Harry Potter books are read by people of all ages.
Italian, French and German are spoken in Switzerland.
The magazine 'Shout' is sold at newsagents all over the country.
The band's new album is advertised on TV and radio.
The advertisements are watched by thousands of people every day.
The role of the hero is played by the actor Joseph Harper.
The soap is filmed in a large school in Manchester.

2 A magazine article
is known; has been turned; have been filmed; were used; was cast; was asked; was flown; was set; has been chosen

3 Making *Last Sunset*
1. was cast
2. told
3. has been advertised
4. was written
5. chose
6. has been used
7. were asked
8. asked

4 From active to passive
a)
2. My mobile phone has been stolen.
3. Francis Herring is known for his horror stories.
4. Kate was told to smile for the camera.
5. The castle was built in 1584.
6. These trees have been cut down.
7. This ad was shown on TV last month.

b)
2. This photo was taken by a German photographer.
3. The glass bowl has been broken by the cat.
4. That picture of me was drawn by my mother.
5. The role of the doctor was played by Henry Forster.
6. Five new trees have been planted by the gardener.
7. The lost dog was found by a twelve-year-old girl.
8. The actors have been chosen by the casting agent.

5 Mediatek Multimedia Centre
2. will be worked on in March
3. will be opened to the general public on April 2nd
4. will be shown to the public
5. will be held on April 12th
6. will be sold on April 25th
7. will be given to charity
8. will be performed on May 1st

6 The past perfect passive
2. hadn't been given
3. hadn't been talked
4. had been cut

5. hadn't been given
6. had been changed
7. hadn't been cleaned
8. had been broken

7 A letter from France
1. was chosen
2. was flown
3. hadn't been told
4. was taken
5. was given
6. are going to be used
7. has been photographed
8. 'll/will be shown
9. 'll/will be looked
10. will be sent

9 Mixed bag: A pirate story
1. was written
2. was given
3. had never been written
4. has just been turned
5. was directed by
6. will be shown
7. will be watched by a lot of people
8. will be finished

Unit 6 Time to travel

1 What did Mina say?
's raining heavily; 'm; feel; has broken; can't; 'm going to be

2 What did Karl say?
was sunbathing; was; could see; had; 'd bought; 'd just had; felt

3 Match the phrases
1. b)
2. c)
3. f)
4. g)
5. d)
6. e)
7. a)

4 What did they actually say?
2. We'll be in New York tomorrow.
3. I'll be back home next week.
4. We've been to the airport this morning.
5. I got your e-mail about the flight yesterday.
6. My cousins are coming to stay here next month.

5 Jacob's letter
hopes; 's been; had; went; can; arrives; can pick us up

6 Karin's exam
if I had; where I was born; if I had ever been; if I could play; if I was going to play

7 Indirect commands
2. warned/advised/ordered me not to touch
3. asked/reminded me to turn
4. advised me to go
5. ordered me to drop
6. asked me to phone
7. allowed me to borrow

8 Harry's trip
2. You should be very careful of the water.
3. Don't forget to take suntan cream.
4. Phone home every day.
5. Don't go swimming on your own.
6. Be careful about pickpockets.
7. And please bring back something for Grandma.

10 Mixed bag: The penguin
he had; had found; a few hours earlier; had looked; was trying; if she had; there was; there; The next day; I'm taking; today

Green Line 4

Lösungen

Unit 1 New York City

1 What's the reason?
1. d)
2. b)
3. a)
4. e)
5. g)
6. f)
7. c)

2 *For* and *since*
a)

For: ages, a few days, the last two months, three weeks, years and years

Since: the summer, he was a child, her last birthday, I was at school, last spring, last Wednesday, yesterday

b)
1. since
2. for

3 Meet Kora
since; For; for; for; since; since; since; for

4 How long have you been doing it?
1. How long have you been going to your school?
2. How long have you been sitting in that chair?
3. How long have you been living in your home?
4. How long have you been learning English?
5. How long have you been doing this exercise?

6 I'd been waiting for hours
2. 'd/had been working
3. 'd/had been living
4. 'd/had been waiting
5. 'd/had been talking
6. hadn't been raining
7. 'd/had been thinking
8. 'd/had been sunbathing

7 Good to see you well!
see (you) well; find (it) hard; makes (me) nervous; called (me) stupid; try (something) safer

8 Adjective or adverb?
1. complete
2. pretty
3. really
4. extreme
5. completely
6. quite
7. amazingly
8. real

9 All about New York City
1. (Visitors to New York ...) often find it difficult to understand the street numbers.
2. (In the winter ...) there is always a big place to skate in Central Park.
3. (Every year ...) in March there is a big festival for Saint Patrick's Day.
4. (In the summer ...) lots of New Yorkers leave the hot city for a few weeks.
5. (There are many ...) art exhibitions held in the city all through the year.
6. (In the spring ...) many tourists come into the gardens to see the trees in flower.

10 Mixed bag: In the museum
had been standing; for; find; interesting; quite; I've been; for

Unit 2 Go, Bears, go!

1 Giving advice
2. You shouldn't have told Kate my secret.
3. You shouldn't have stopped to buy a magazine.
4. You should have remembered the right exercise.
5. You shouldn't have left your dad's mobile phone on the bus.
6. You shouldn't have watched that film.
7. You shouldn't have got bad marks./You should have got better marks.

2 Good listeners
1. f)
2. d)
3. c)
4. b)
5. a)
6. e)

3 You needn't have done that!
2. You needn't have gone to all that trouble.
3. I needn't have sent him that e-mail.
4. We needn't have learnt them by heart.
5. They needn't have bought a new one.
6. I needn't have watered the plants this morning.

4 Trouble at school
might; shouldn't; must; might; can't; shouldn't; should; might not

5 Where could I have left it?
might/must have left; can't have done; must/could/might have put; might/must/could have done; must/might have forgotten; should have been; might/could have found; must have closed; might have picked; should/might/could have thought

6 The passive infinitive
2. to be called
3. to be allowed
4. to be given
5. to be told
6. to be made
7. to be finished
8. to be shown

7 Lucy's Saturday job
The vegetables need/have to be cut up.
The rubbish needs/has to be taken out.
The tables need/have to be laid.
The flowers need/have to be put on the tables.
The glasses need/have to be polished.
The menu board needn't/doesn't have to be written.

8 He should be told!
2. Your bike might be stolen if you leave it there.
3. The teacher should be told what's been happening.
4. This classroom shouldn't be used for the next 24 hours.
5. A new swimming pool might be built at school next year. (It has just been painted.)
6. Computer games can be borrowed from the new library.

9 Mixed bag: Modal auxiliaries and the passive
a)
1. needn't/shouldn't
2. must
3. shouldn't
4. could/would/might

b)
1. might be accepted
2. might have left
3. to be paid
4. could have walked
5. should have bought
6. can be found
7. to be cleaned
8. to be finished

Unit 3 Out West

1 From coast to coast
Travelling across the States; Looking out of the window; Reading and writing in English; Sitting for hours talking with a stranger; Being able to speak naturally to people in English; Taking pictures from a moving train; Getting from the East coast to the West coast

2 Travelling on Route 66
2. Driving across the States is a great way to get to know the country.
3. Spending time with real American people is the best way to learn the language.

4. Being able to swim in the sea for six months a year is the thing I love about Florida.
5. Knowing how to make polite conversation is an important part of learning English.
6. Losing my passport was the scariest part of my trip.

3 Rodeo!
watching; kicking; going; hanging; doing; hurting; falling; taking; seeing

4 Do you like the music playing on the radio?
2. my neighbour's dog barking all night
3. people telling me what to do
4. Jane coming home
5. your computer making that funny noise
6. my little sister borrowing all my things
7. my cousins visiting me tomorrow

5 Polite requests
2. the dog being
3. the children shouting
4. the elevator not working
5. the rain coming down
6. my cousin coming to stay

6 Joshua Tree National Park
was created; was made; is visited; have been written; will be built; to be enjoyed; are not allowed; are asked

7 From active to passive
1. A new shopping mall is being built next to our school.
2. When I saw the building, part of it was being cleaned.
3. A movie was being filmed at the park during our visit.
4. On the news we saw a man being rescued by a helicopter.

9 In the right order
1. The statue was paid for by the members of the City Theatre.
2. I don't like being looked at by large groups of people.
3. I feel badly let down by Mike.
4. The island has been fought over by five different countries this century.
5. Celebrities are used to being written about in the newspapers.

10 Mixed bag: Visiting Phoenix
travelling; used; going; getting; being; cooking; being; was; be; swimming; been

Unit 4 Extreme action

1 A postcard home
promise; come; get; stop; cross; to jump; be; to stop; to get; to see; say

2 Stay on the paths!
warn you not to pick; need you all to stay; tell you not to get; ask you not to take; don't want anyone to get

3 Jumbled sentences
1. Nobody expected Sam to do so well in the competition.
2. Where do you want me to put these books?
3. Do you expect me to climb up there?
4. I want you to know how pleased I am to win this award.
5. Would you prefer me to e-mail you or to phone you?
6. The instructors advised us to take warm clothes.

4 Lizzie's trip
2. to take a camera with her
3. kind of bag to take with her
4. money to take with her
5. time of year to go
6. to buy a good map of the area
7. to ask about the best routes

5 A 75th birthday party
the first to arrive; the best person to have; the next to get; the last to find out; the youngest to go; the oldest woman in the country to do; the best way to make

7 Find the mistakes
1. I'd like be able to drive because I hate have to walk to school in the rain.
   correct version: I'd **like to be able to** drive because I **hate having to/to have to** walk to school in the rain.
2. Thanks for the offer help, but I think I prefer to doing it myself.
   correct version: Thanks for the **offer to help**, but I think I **prefer doing/to do** it myself.
3. It's started rain again so our idea of to go to the beach will have to wait until tomorrow.
   correct version: It's **started raining/to rain** again so our **idea of going** to the beach will have to wait until tomorrow.
4. I like watching other people to do dangerous things but I'm not interested in to do them myself.
   correct version: I like watching other people **do/doing** dangerous things but I'm not **interested in doing** them myself.
5. I'm used to get up early, but now the days have started get so short it's harder for me.
   correct version: I'm **used to getting up** early, but now the days **have started getting/to get** so short it's harder for me.
6. My brother loves to watching TV in the evening, but I prefer to reading.
   correct version: My brother **loves watching/to watch** TV in the evening, but I **prefer reading/to read**.

8 Gerund or infinitive?
1. calling
2. walking
3. to buy
4. climbing
5. to jump
6. to win
7. raining
8. to break

9 Mixed bag: Camp tales
1. looking
2. to have climbed
3. how many
4. to telling
5. to take
6. to bring

7. to hurt
8. keep
9. to make
10. walking
11. whether
12. to put
13. go
14. to find
15. helping
16. how
17. to get
18. to bring

Unit 5 The Golden State

1 Defining or non-defining

1. non-defining: The film Angels in Waiting, which stars Johnny Weiss, comes out next Friday.
2. non-defining: My youngest sister, who loves everything to do with Hollywood, has asked me to photograph Sunset Boulevard.
3. defining
4. non-defining: Brian Horowitz, who lives near Palm Beach, is a great surfer.
5. defining
6. non-defining: The swimsuit I bought last week, which was reduced in the sale, fit me perfectly.
7. defining
8. non-defining: The San Francisco earthquake of 1906, in which around 3,000 people died, is the worst in the history of the city.
9. defining
10. non-defining: The best hotel we stayed in, which was near Venice Beach, had a great view of the sea.

2 Which relative pronoun?

1. whose
2. which
3. which
4. which
5. who
6. which
7. whose
8. who

3 The Walk of Fame

d; a; g; e; b; h; c; f

4 All about the Golden State

Silicon Valley, which is where many of the world's largest technology companies have their home, is in the San Francisco Bay area.
Richard Nixon, who was President of the United States from 1969 to 1974, was born in Yorba Linda, California.
The Gold Rush in 1849 brought thousands of people, who were later called the forty-niners, into the state of California in 1849.
Ernest and Julio Gallo, whose wine company is now the largest exporter of Californian wines, started the company in 1933.
Mountains, which cover a large area of the state of California, often have snow on them all year long.

5 The surfing goat

2. which is popular with local surfers
3. which is called Goatee
4. who were watching Dayna and his friends surfing
5. which amazed me
6. who had brought a camera
7. which was also shown on TV
8. who had bought the goat five months ago
9. where he used to live

7 California facts

1. California, which is called *The Golden State*, is one of the top tourist places in the US.
2. More than 300 tons of grapes, which grow easily in California, are grown every year.
3. The first ever cinema in the world, which was called *Tally's Electric Theater*, opened in L.A. in 1902.
4. The Beach Boys, who were a popular band in the 1960s, made California internationally famous.
5. In 1854 the largest piece of gold ever found, which weighed 195 pounds, was discovered in California.

8 Past or present participle?

1. Breathing
2. Built
3. Carrying
4. enjoyed
5. Feeling
6. forgotten
7. Opened
8. wanting
9. holding
10. posted

9 Mixed bag: What should you do in an earthquake?

where I was living at the time; which only lasted for about 20 seconds; which was full of food; falling off the shelves; safely attached to the wall; which often happens after an earthquake; which will protect you from falling objects; broken glass; which might fall down and hurt you; where you are safer from falling trees